SOVIET TRADE UNIONS

SOVIET
TRADE UNIONS

THEIR PLACE
IN SOVIET LABOUR POLICY

by

ISAAC DEUTSCHER

HYPERION PRESS, INC.
WESTPORT, CONNECTICUT

Library of Congress Cataloging in Publication Data

Deutscher, Isaac, 1907-1967.
  Soviet trade unions.

  Reprint of the 1950 ed. published by Oxford
University Press, London.
    1. Trade-unions--Russia. 2. Labor policy--
Russia. I. Title.
HD6732.D4 1973   331.88'0947   73-837
  ISBN 0-88355-033-4

Published in 1950
by Oxford University Press, London, England

First Hyperion reprint edition 1973

Library of Congress Catalogue Number 73-837

ISBN 0-88355-033-4

Printed in the United States of America

Contents

PREFACE   vii

1. TRADE UNIONS UNDER TSARDOM   1
   Lenin on Trade Unions   2
   Trade Unions in the 1905 Revolution and After   8

2. TRADE UNIONS AND THE REVOLUTION   13
   After the October Revolution   17
   Debates at the First Trade Union Congress   18
   Trade Unions in the Civil War   25
   'Point Five' of the 1919 Programme   28
   Individual Management and Labour Armies   33
   The Trade Union Controversy at the Tenth
     Party Congress: 42
     (a) The Views of Trotsky-Bukharin   43
     (b) The Workers' Opposition   46
     (c) 'Platform of Ten'   48
   Proletarian Dictatorship, Proletarian Demo-
     cracy, and Trade Unions   52

3. THE NEW ECONOMIC POLICY   59
   Transition to NEP   59
   Trade Unions under NEP   66

4. PLANNED ECONOMY   75
   Transition to Planned Economy   76
   Trade Unions and Planned Economy   81
     (a) Industrial Recruitment   84
     (b) Training of Labour   93
     (c) 'Socialist Emulation'   96
     (d) Wages Policy   100
     (e) Stakhanovism   109
     (f) Trade Unions and Social Insurance   116

v

CONTENTS

5. MACHINERY AND ORGANIZATION OF TRADE
   UNIONS   121

6. THE TENTH TRADE UNION CONGRESS   128

7. ROAD TO SERFDOM?   135

APPENDIX
   Statute of the Soviet Trade Unions   141

INDEX   153

Preface

THIS essay attempts to describe and analyse the role and outlook of the Soviet trade unions, the various phases of their evolution since the Bolshevik upheaval of 1917, and the functions they have performed in the planned economy of the U.S.S.R. It also attempts to explain to what extent the Soviet trade unions defend or fail to defend the interests of their members *vis-à-vis* the employer-State and in what relation they stand towards the Communist Party.

The material for this monograph has been drawn mainly from Russian sources such as the verbatim reports of the Congresses of Soviet Trade Unions and of the Communist Party, the Russian trade union press, and the decrees and resolutions of Government and party bearing on labour policy. The viewpoints expressed by oppositions of every shade are discussed here alongside the official Soviet attitudes. Soviet literature on this subject provided a wealth of information throughout the first decade or so after the revolution, when trade unionism was often the subject of dramatic controversy inside the Bolshevik Party, although even then the facts and data published were not always reliable. Since the late nineteen-twenties, however, the sources of information have been progressively drying up. The monolithic nature of the regime has precluded any frank and honest discussion of this as of most other issues. Stalinist orthodoxy, propagandist distortion, and habitual secrecy have combined to surround even so utterly prosaic an institution as the trade unions with a thick web of legend and myth.

This web, however, has every now and then been brushed aside for a moment by the rude fist of administrative or economic necessity, which has compelled Government and party to issue decrees, instructions, or orders regulating the work of the trade unions, These decrees and instructions, especially when they are read and analysed in the light of preceding controversies, those that took place in the nineteen-twenties, help the student to obtain a picture of the real structure and functions of the trade unions.

The limitations of the source materials that are available make it impossible at present to attempt a comprehensive history of Soviet trade unions. This monograph does not pretend to offer a systematic historical narrative. The documentation is enough to enable us to record and analyse the crucial features of the trade unions and to define their place in Soviet labour policy. From this description and analysis the reader should be able to gauge to what extent the Soviet trade unions have developed away from, not only the patterns of trade unionism outside the U.S.S.R., but also from the standards once set for it by the Bolshevik leaders themselves. This 'deviation' has reflected more than the arbitrary whims of the leaders, even though there has been no lack of arbitrary decisions and practices. The functions of Soviet 'trade unionism' have been organically connected with the peculiar type of planned economy which has grown up, or has been built up, in the economically primitive and socially backward environment of the Soviet Union since the late nineteen-twenties. Only in the context of that economy and that environment can the strange evolution of the trade unions be understood. The author has therefore been compelled occasionally to stray away, at least seemingly, from his proper topic into the vast field of general Soviet economics, but he has tried to limit such excursions to the minimum consistent with the nature of the subject and its understanding.

A few words of explanation are perhaps needed about the manner in which the various phases of Soviet trade unionism have been treated. The trends that came to light in the early years of the Soviet regime are discussed in greater detail than subsequent developments, so that the reader may get the impression of a certain chronological incongruity. Unfortunately, this could not be avoided. It is not only that the documentation on the early years is more abundant; those years were also in every sense the formative period of Soviet trade unionism. It was then that conflicting theories of labour policy and conceptions of trade unionism openly clashed in public debate. Some of those theories and conceptions were very shrewd, if not fully conscious, anticipations of the present condition of Soviet trade unionism. In later years the whole issue was drowned in floods of dull, uninformative propaganda. Thus, the stormy trade union debates of 1921–2 still tell us much more about the principle underlying the present outlook of the trade unions than do the reports of their most recent Congress, that of April 1949. It is therefore proper to keep the searchlight closer and longer on some nearly forgotten but still highly instructive episodes than on a recent event from which we can learn very little. Incidentally, the full significance of the early formative phases of Soviet trade unionism has become apparent only in the light of much later developments; and so far it has not been critically analysed in that light either in the Soviet Union or elsewhere. For these reasons, chronological balance has up to a point been sacrificed to the analytical purpose of this study.

I should like to express my thanks to the research and library staff of the Royal Institute of International Affairs, and especially to Mrs Jane Degras and Mrs Margaret Dewar, who have read my manuscript and have offered their helpful criticisms.

1

Trade Unions under Tsardom

ONE of the striking features of the Russian labour movement before the revolution of 1917 was the relative
insignificance of the trade unions. In part, this was
due to the fact that Russian industry was still very young and
that the mass of industrial workers consisted of recently proletarianized peasants. The trade unions of western Europe had
behind them the long tradition of medieval guilds, whose
descendants in a sense they were. No such tradition existed in
Russia. More important still, up to the beginning of this
century trade union organization was as strictly prohibited
and persecuted by tsardom as was any form of political opposition. In suppressing trade unionism, tsardom unwittingly
put a premium upon revolutionary political organization.[1]
Only the most politically-minded workers, those prepared to
pay for their conviction with prison and exile, could be willing
to join trade unions in these circumstances. But those who
were already so politically-minded were, naturally enough,
more attracted by political organizations. The broader and
more inert mass of workers, who were inclined to shun politics
but would have readily joined trade unions, were not only
prevented from forming unions but were also gradually accustomed to look for leadership to the clandestine political
parties. 'The most characteristic feature in the history of our
Trade Unions,' says Stalin, 'is that they have emerged, developed and grown strong only after the party, around the

[1] In 1902 Col Zubatov, chief of the Moscow political police, sponsored
closely-supervised trade unions designed to compete with the revolutionary
organizations. These police-sponsored trade unions were no substitute for
real ones; and they were soon infiltrated by the revolutionaries.

party and in friendship with the party.' This view, somewhat over-simple, is, nevertheless, essentially correct. Whereas in Britain the Labour Party was created by the trade unions, the Russian trade unions from their beginning led their existence in the shadow of the political movement. Although sporadic economic associations of workers occurred as early as in the eighties and even seventies of the last century, it is, broadly speaking, true that the political organization, more specifically the Russian Social Democratic Workers' Party, and not the trade unions, held the birthright in the Russian labour movement.

LENIN ON TRADE UNIONS

Revolutionary socialist politics did not, however, gain ascendancy over the economic movement without some struggle. In 1899 a group of socialists, who were soon labelled 'Economists', set out to dispute the supremacy of revolutionary politics. For a short time they did so with some success; they found strong support even among underground circles of socialists. But their success was shortlived. By 1903, when the Social Democratic Party held its second Congress, at which it split into Bolsheviks and Mensheviks, the influence of the 'Economists' had already waned. Among the Social Democrats who preached the primacy of revolutionary politics, the young Lenin played a very prominent role. In his polemical writings against the 'Economists' he first developed his views on trade unionism, views which he was to hold, in almost unmodified form, up to 1917. Even after 1917 his approach to trade unions was in the main governed by the broad view of the inter-relationship of economics and politics, class, party and trade unions, which he had expressed in those early polemics. It is therefore worthwhile briefly to survey Lenin's ideas on the subject:

When . . . the first International was formed, the question of the significance of the Trade Unions and of the workers' economic struggle was raised at its first Congress in Geneva in 1866. The resolution of that Congress underlined with precision the significance of the economic struggle, warning socialists and workers, on the one hand, against overrating its importance (which was characteristic for the English workers at that time) and, on the other, against underrating it (which was characteristic for the French and the Germans, especially the followers of Lassalle). The resolution recognized that Trade Unions were not only legitimate but necessary as long as capitalism existed; it recognized them to be extremely important in the organization of the working class in its daily struggle against capital and for the abolition of wage labour. The resolution also stated that Trade Unions ought not to pay their attention exclusively to 'the direct struggle against capital', that they ought not to keep aloof from the political and social movement of the working class. They ought not to pursue 'narrow' objectives, but they ought to strive for the general emancipation of the oppressed millions of the working people. . . The conviction that the single class struggle ought necessarily to unite the political and the economic struggle has become part and parcel of the international social democratic outlook.[1]

The attitude of the 'Economists' was by no means uniform or clear-cut. Some of them were opposed to the creation of a political Social Democratic Party; others merely urged the party, then in its first formative period, to base its policy exclusively or primarily on the immediate economic interests of the workers. Against this Lenin argued that (a) the party should, of course, base its activity *inter alia* on the workers' immediate economic interests, and (b) that those interests formed a highly inadequate basis for the party's policy as a whole:

For the socialist the economic struggle serves as the basis for the organization of workers in a revolutionary party, for the consolidation and development of the class struggle against the whole capitalist system. But if the economic struggle is regarded as something self-sufficient, then there is nothing socialist in it. And in the experience of all European countries we have had many not only socialist but also anti-socialist Trade Unions.

'To assist in the economic struggle of the proletariat' [this was what the 'Economists' wanted]—is the job of the bourgeois politician. The task of the socialist is to make the economic struggle of the workers assist the socialist movement and contribute to the success of the revolutionary socialist party.[2]

The entire Leninist conception of proletarian class struggle

[1] Lenin, *Sochinenia* (Works), 4th ed. (Moscow, in progress), IV, 158-9.
[2] ibid. IV, 270.

3

was implied in this deliberately paradoxical epigram. Lenin saw the working class as a heterogeneous mass consisting of the most diverse elements and representing the most diverse levels of 'class-consciousness'. Various groups of workers are immediately interested merely in securing their own, narrow, material advantage. They may try to secure it against the interests of other groups of workers, an attitude characteristic of craft trade unionism. Other groups may try to secure immediate advantages at the expense even of their own long-term interests. Sections of the working class thus try to assert themselves against the rest of the class; and at times even the whole working class sacrifices its collective and permanent interests for the sake of meretricious and transitory benefits. It was true in Lenin's view, as Marx had pointed out, that modern industry tended to organize the proletariat for class struggle, to shape its collective mind and to discipline its will; but it was also true that the unity of the working class was being constantly disrupted by centrifugal forces, that its class consciousness was constantly disintegrating, and that its collective will was being dissipated in the pursuit of the most diverse and contradictory objectives.

This dialectical contradiction between the unifying and the disruptive tendencies formed the background against which Lenin viewed the respective roles of various labour organizations, and analysed the relative antagonism between trade unionism and political socialism. It was the peculiar task of the Socialist (and later of the Communist) Party to unify the proletariat for the pursuit of its corporate and permanent interest—the overthrow of capitalism and the establishment of socialism. To this objective the party had to subordinate the sectional or temporary interests of the working class. It was, on the other hand, inherent in trade unionism that it should devote its energy to the workers' sectional and temporary advantages.

4

From this fundamental difference in the functions of trade union and party followed the profound differences in the outlook and structure of the two organizations. The trade union tended to embrace the bulk of the working class. It was a mass organization *par excellence*. The party, on the other hand, ought to embrace only the most advanced, class conscious, and disciplined elements of the class. It was, or should be an *élite* organization, for only such an *élite*, closely-knit and politically-trained, could be the unifying and leading factor in the life of the working class. In this sense the Socialist Party was the 'vanguard of the proletariat'.

By definition the party embraced only a minority, perhaps a very small one, of the working class. It would be contrary to its nature and functions for it to try to embrace the majority —this would mean that the *élite* of the class had become 'dissolved' in the amorphous mass. It was only in 1903, when the Russian Social Democracy split into Bolsheviks and Mensheviks, that Lenin dotted the i's and crossed the t's of this theory, but he expounded its essential tenets even in the earlier years.

At first sight this conception resembled various older theories of 'active minorities' or groups of revolutionary initiative, of which Blanquism had been the best known. Lenin was, indeed, charged with following in the footsteps of Blanqui and expounded the idea of a revolution accomplished by a small minority. The resemblance, he replied, was superficial. Blanqui believed in revolution accomplished by a conspiratorial *élite*, without the participation, and regardless of the attitude, of the majority of the nation. Not so Lenin. His *élite* or the proletarian vanguard, organized in the party, was not called upon to make the revolution by itself. Its task was to persuade, prepare, and organize the vast majority of the nation for the upheaval. Socialist revolution could win and succeed only if it was approved and supported by the majority;

5

but that majority had to be enlightened and guided by a class-conscious Marxist minority. In periods of reaction or slow social development the party might be isolated from the working class. But in the process of revolution it would assume the actual leadership of the broadest masses of the working people.

In the light of this theory, the relationship between party and trade unions could not be free from some dualism. The Marxist vanguard must not turn its back upon the trade unions. Since its purpose was to influence and lead the mass of the workers, it had, on the contrary, to turn to the trade unions, in which that mass was organized; but it could turn to them only in the sense in which the leader turns to the led. In no circumstances could it place itself on an equal footing with the trade unions—this would amount to a renunciation of its own peculiar mission. It was the task of the party to see to it that the struggle for 'bread and butter', led by the trade unions, should not deflect the workers from, but that it should prepare them for the revolutionary transformation of society. As long as the trade unions were willing to be guided along that path, their role was, from the party's viewpoint, progressive. As soon, however, as they proclaimed their 'neutrality' in politics, or, what was worse, the primacy of their narrowly economic pursuits, the party inevitably came in conflict with them, for the trade unions were now in fact reconciling themselves with the existing social order. From the Marxist viewpoint, their struggle for 'bread and butter' could, anyhow, not be effective in the long run, for even if they succeeded in obtaining higher wages or better labour conditions for their workers, the share of the working class in the national income was in the longer run bound to decline as long as capitalism existed.

Social Democracy [wrote Lenin in the first issue of *Iskra* in December 1900] represents the unification of the [labour] movement with socialism.

6

Its task is not to serve passively the labour movement . . . but to represent the interests of the movement as a whole, to put before that movement its final objective. . . . Severed from Social Democracy, the labour movement grows insignificant and inevitably acquires a bourgeois outlook: waging the economic struggle only, the working class loses its political independence, becomes an appendage to other parties and betrays the high principle that 'the emancipation of the workers should be achieved by the workers themselves'. In all countries there was a time when the labour movement and socialism existed separately and moved along separate roads—and in all countries this divorce led to the weakness of socialism and of the labour movement alike. . .[1]

When one of Lenin's opponents argued that Social Democracy should give up pure politics and try to lend a political character to the economic struggle (this was another shade of 'Economism'), Lenin replied:

The economic struggle is a collective struggle of the workers against their employers for better terms *in the sale of their labour power*, for better conditions of life and labour. This is inevitably a Trade Union struggle, because the conditions of labour differ greatly from trade to trade. . . 'To lend a political character to the economic struggle' means consequently to strive for the realization of these same Trade Union demands . . . 'by way of legislative and administrative measures' . . . This exactly is what all Trade Unions have been and are doing. Look into the work of the solid scholars (and solid opportunists) Mr and Mrs Webb, and you will see that the English Trade Unions have long since recognized . . . the task of 'lending a political character to the economic struggle' . . . Thus behind this pompous phrase . . . there is in fact the customary attempt to lower Social Democratic policy to the level of Trade Unionism! . . .

Revolutionary Social Democracy has always included and still includes the fight for reforms in its activities. But it makes use of 'economic' agitation in order to confront the government not only with demands for all sorts of measures, but also (and primarily) with the demand that this government cease to be an autocracy. . . In a word, Social Democracy subordinates the struggle for reforms to the revolutionary struggle for freedom and socialism in the same way in which any part is subordinate to the whole.[2]

In this same polemic Lenin emphasized another crucial difference between party and trade unions. The trade union is strictly a workers' organization, whereas the party concerns

[1] Lenin, *Sochinenia*, IV, 343.   [2] ibid. v, 474–6.

7

itself with the condition of all social classes. The central figure in the Social Democratic Party is not and should not be the man with the outlook of a trade union secretary but the tribune of the people.

. . . the 'Economists' always lapse from Social Democracy back into *Trade Unionism*.[1] The political struggle waged by Social Democrats is far more extensive and complex than the economic struggle of the workers against the employers and the government. Similarly, the organization of a Revolutionary Social Democratic Party must inevitably *differ* from the organizations of the workers for economic struggle. A workers' organization must in the first place be a trade organization; secondly, it must be as wide as possible; and, thirdly, there must be as little clandestinity about it as possible. (Here and farther I have, of course, only autocratic Russia in mind.) On the contrary, the organization of revolutionaries ought to embrace first of all and mainly people for whom their revolutionary activity is their [main] occupation. . . In view of this common characteristic of the members of such an organization, *every distinction between workers and intellectuals ought to vanish*, not to speak of distinctions between occupations . . .[2]

TRADE UNIONS IN THE 1905 REVOLUTION AND AFTER

The supremacy of revolutionary politics over trade unionism became apparent in the first Russian revolution of 1905. The tsarist autocracy was greatly weakened; and the trade unions, for the first time enjoying full freedom of organization, gained considerable membership. Nevertheless, their role in the turbulent strike movement of that year was only secondary. In St Petersburg, the capital and the centre of the revolution, they were completely overshadowed by a new institution that had spontaneously sprung into being—the Council of Workers' Delegates, the first Soviet in history. So, incidentally, were also the political parties, some of which,

[1] Lenin uses the English expression 'trade unionism' in the Russian text to denote the negative aspects of the trade unionist's attitude. In this pejorative sense the English expression has ever since been used by Russian Bolshevik writers.

[2] Lenin, *Sochinenia*, v, 421–2.

8

especially the Bolsheviks, were at first vaguely opposed to the Soviet. It was this Council of Workers' Delegates that actually inspired the great general strike of November 1905, which, together with the December rising in Moscow, marked the culmination of the revolution. Even the campaign for the eight hours' day was proclaimed primarily by the Soviet.

The auxiliary role of the trade unions was emphasized in a resolution adopted by the Fourth Congress of the Russian Social Democratic Workers' Party (April and May 1906), at which Bolsheviks and Mensheviks reunited into a single party. The resolution stated that 'in the atmosphere of a revolutionary epoch the trade unions, apart from defending the economic interests of the workers, draw the working class into direct political struggle and assist in its broad organization and political unification.'[1] The Congress obliged all members of the party to join trade unions and participate in their work; but, curiously enough, it pronounced itself in favour of setting up 'non-party' trade unions. (This was the common view of Bolsheviks and Mensheviks, since the clause about the non-party character of the trade unions can be found in the Bolshevik motion which was not passed by the Congress.) At the same time the Congress rejected any notion of political neutrality of the unions.

A comparison between the resolution passed by the Congress and the Bolshevik motion discloses one significant difference. The Bolsheviks insisted that the party ought to do its utmost to secure its actual leadership in the non-party unions, whereas the general resolution spoke vaguely about the need for an 'organic connexion' between party and unions. The same Congress adopted a brief resolution against the division of the unions along the lines of nationality. The trade union ought to embrace workers regardless of nationality,

[1] *V.K.P. (b) o Profsoyuzakh* (All-Union Communist Party on Trade Unions) 2nd ed. (Moscow, 1940), pp. 12–13.

9

creed, race, etc. The difficulty which was to split the trade union movement in the Austro-Hungarian empire along the lines of nationality was from the beginning solved in an internationalist spirit in Russia.

The relationship between party and trade unions underwent some change after 1906, in the years of counter-revolution, under the so-called regime of the 3 June. For quite a few years the political parties were wrecked and demoralized by defeat. The Mensheviks never succeeded in reconstituting a solid clandestine organization; the Bolsheviks did so only slowly and with great difficulty. The regime of 3 June did not spare the trade unions either. Many unions were banned; their members were severely punished for participation in strikes or other economic activity. But some trade unions were allowed to exist under close police supervision. This soon gave rise to hesitation in the ranks of the Social Democratic Party. The so-called 'Liquidators' among the Mensheviks (those who were prepared to give up clandestine political organization altogether) were inclined to confine themselves to such forms of activity as were tolerated by the Government. They were consequently ready to accept virtually non-political trade unions. At the London Congress of the party, in 1907, an attempt was made to revise the party's attitude towards trade unions. A motion[1] tabled at the Congress stated that 'the premature establishment of an organizational connexion [between the Social Democratic Party and the Trade Unions] may result . . . in separation and alienation between the political and the economic organizations of the proletariat . . . on the other hand, as experience has shown, the Trade Unions which are neutral *vis-à-vis* the parties have, in the overwhelming majority of cases, adhered to a class policy and have not held aloof from the general

[1] *V.K.P.* (*b*) *v Rezolutsiyakh* (Resolutions of the All-Union Communist Party) 5th ed. (Moscow, 1936), I, pp. 116–17.

proletarian movement.' The practical conclusion was that the Social Democrats should give up their aspiration to lead the trade unions wherever their insistence on this threatened to weaken the unions. This attempt to revise the party's attitude brought forth a sharp protest from Lenin. The Congress was unable to reach a conclusion; and the four resolutions on the matter submitted to the Congress were not put to the vote.

Soon afterwards, the joint Bolshevik-Menshevik Central Committee of the party restated its attitude in a manner which, on the whole, conformed with Lenin's attitude. The idea of neutral trade unions was once again ruled out of court. The party was, on the other hand, warned that it should not try to impose itself upon the unions; it should rather secure its influence by way of solid propaganda and organization; and it should exercise that influence so as not to weaken the unity of the trade unionists in their economic struggle. Acknowledging that the Government of the 3 June had succeeded in routing many or most of the trade unions, the Central Committee pointed out that this was due to the fact that the unions had failed to build up strong nuclei within the factories and the workshops. To withstand further repression they should be firmly anchored in the factories and workshops. The Social Democratic Party, on the other hand, ought to form its own nuclei within those wider trade union nuclei in the factories.[1]

This resolution, endorsed by both Bolsheviks and Mensheviks in February 1908, suggested the pattern for the so-called 'fractions' and cells which later were to become characteristic for the Communist method of organization. At the bottom of the organizational pyramid there is the broad mass of workers, many of them inert or backward; the more advanced or active part of that mass is organized in trade

[1] *V.K.P. (b) o Profsoyuzakh*, pp. 30–1.

11

unions and leads the rest, especially in times of economic conflict with employers and or with the Government; within the trade union the most politically-minded and organized elements form the party cell, which should, thanks to its moral authority, superior experience and skill, guide the trade unions directly or indirectly; the activities of the party cells in their turn are guided and co-ordinated, directly or indirectly, by the leadership of the party. Thus the leadership of the party should be able to exercise—through a whole series of intermediate links—its influence upon the broadest masses. (At a later period the trade unions were to be called the 'transmission belts' between the party and the main body of the working class.)

In subsequent years this scheme of organization could not be put into operation on any wide scale. The labour movement was in a state of depression until roughly 1912, when a political revival manifested itself in many strikes. This revival was for a time interrupted by the outbreak of the First World War.

2

Trade Unions and the Revolution

THE effect of the revolution which took place in February 1917 was in one way similar to that of the revolution of 1905: the newly-won political freedom favoured the rapid growth of the trade unions. In 1905 the trade unions counted 250,000 members. During the first months of 1917 their membership rose from a few scores of thousands to 1·5 million. These numbers reflected the general urge of workers to use the newly-won freedom of organization.

The practical role of the trade unions in the revolution did not, however, correspond to their numerical strength. It was even less significant than in 1905. For one thing, in 1917 strikes never assumed the scale and power they had in 1905. The economic ruin of Russia, the galloping inflation, the scarcity of consumers' goods, and so on, made normal 'bread and butter' struggle look unreal. In addition, the threat of mobilization hung over would-be strikers. The working class was in no mood to strive for limited economic advantages and partial reforms. The entire social order of Russia was at stake. Even more than in 1905 the trade unions were now overshadowed by the Soviets, and at no significant turn of the revolution did they come to the fore.

As in all labour organizations, so in the unions the extreme and the moderate parties—Bolsheviks, Mensheviks, and Social Revolutionaries—confronted one another in a ceaseless and intense struggle for influence. At first the trade unions, like the Soviets, were dominated by the Mensheviks, who nominally favoured the trade unions' political neutrality. On behalf of the Labour Ministry of the Kerensky Government,

13

Maisky (the future Soviet ambassador in London, then still a Menshevik) claimed to guide the trade unions in this spirit.[1] The claim was not very strongly based on the facts: under Menshevik leadership the trade unions supported the Kerensky Government and his war policy. The Menshevik advocacy of neutrality was mainly a form of their opposition to the growth of Bolshevik influence in the trade unions.

As they were preparing for the seizure of power, Lenin and his followers tried to approach the trade unions from a new angle and to define their role in the Soviet system. The central economic idea which Lenin then expounded was 'workers' control' over industry. This did not yet amount to wholesale socialization or nationalization of the economy. 'Workers' control' was to be a sort of dual control of employers and workers over industry, a condominium in which the workers were to train themselves for future exclusive management and in which they were progressively to widen the sphere of their responsibility. Lenin did not envisage any prolonged collaboration between the classes; and his 'workers' control' can therefore not be compared with, say, the British joint production committees. 'Workers' control', on the contrary, provided the framework for the struggle between capitalists and workers in a transition period, at the end of which the former were to be expropriated. The trade unions were expected to play their part in establishing 'workers' control'.

A resolution of the Bolshevik Central Committee, passed some time before the October revolution, contained the following scheme of the control:[2]

For such control it is necessary: (1) that in all important establishments there should be secured for the workers a majority of not less than three

[1] *1. Vserossiiskii Syezd Profsoyuzov* (First All-Russian Congress of Trade Unions; Moscow, 1918), p. 10.
[2] *V.K.P. (b) o Profsoyuzakh*, p. 62.

14

quarters of all votes. It is thereby obligatory to draw into participation the industrialists who have not deserted their businesses and the educated technical and scientific personnel; (2) that the factory committees, the central and local Councils of Workers', Peasants, and Soldiers' Delegates and the Trade Unions should obtain the right to participate in control, that all commercial books and bank accounts should be opened to them and all data obligatorily supplied to them; and (3) that representatives of all influential democratic and socialist parties should obtain the same rights.

From these terms it is clear that the dual power of capitalists and workers in industry was designed to end in the complete elimination of the former—very few capitalists could be expected to reconcile themselves to a situation in which at least three-quarters of the controlling votes belonged to the workers.

Another significant point is the order in which the various labour organizations participating in 'workers' control' were enumerated: the factory committees came first, then the Soviets, and only in the last instance the trade unions. This order corresponded to the actual importance which the three types of organization had in the economic upheaval, as distinct from the political revolution in which the Soviets came first.

The factory committees constituted the most direct representation of the workers and employees of any factory and workshop. They were the primary and basic units of organization, much narrower than the trade unions or the Soviets, but of much greater weight in the establishment of workers' control. The struggle for that control was waged within every factory or workshop of any significance, and its immediate purpose was control by the workers 'on the spot'. At this stage the Bolsheviks appeared as adherents of the most extreme decentralization of economic power, which gave their Menshevik opponents the opportunity to charge them with abandoning Marxism in favour of anarchism. Actually, Lenin and his followers remained firm upholders of the Marxist conception of the centralized State. Their immediate objective, however, was not yet to set up the centralized proletarian dictatorship but to decentralize as much as possible the bourgeois State and the bourgeois economy. This was a necessary condition for the success of the revolution. In the economic field, therefore, the factory committee, the organ 'on the spot', rather than the trade union, was the most potent and deadly instrument of upheaval. Thus the trade unions were relegated to the background not only by the Soviets but also by the factory committees.[1]

Another body which stole the trade unions' thunder was the Workers' Section of the Soviet. This consisted of those members of the Soviet who had been directly elected in factories and workshops. The Workers' Section often held

[1] At the first All-Russian conference of factory committees which opened a few days before the October revolution, Schmidt, the future Commissar for Labour in Lenin's Government, stated: 'At the moment when the factory committees were formed the Trade Unions actually did not yet exist, and the factory committees filled the vacuum.' Later on, after the trade unions gained in strength, 'control from below' was exercised by the factory committees. (See *Oktyabrskaya Revolutsiya i Fabzavkomy* [The October Revolution and the Factory Committees] Moscow, 1927, II, 188.) Another speaker stated at the conference: '. . . the growth of the influence of the factory committees has naturally occurred at the expense of centralized economic organizations of the working class such as the Trade Unions. . . This, of course, is a highly abnormal development which has in practice led to very undesirable results. . . .' ibid. p. 190. Against this an anarchist speaker argued: 'The Trade Unions wish to devour the factory committees. There is no popular discontent with the factory committees, but there is discontent with the Trade Unions. . . To the workers the Trade Union is a form of organization imposed from without. The factory committee is closer to them. . . Anarchists think that they should set up and develop the cells of future society. . . The factory committees are such cells of the future. . . They, not the state, will now administer . . .' ibid. p. 191. The anarchist influence in the factory committees was fairly strong at that time, but the antagonism between Bolshevism and anarchism was still largely hidden. In the first half of 1917 the Mensheviks, dominating the trade unions, tried in vain to bring the factory committees under control. The Bolsheviks then juxtaposed the factory committees to the trade unions and so they had some common ground with the anarchists. ibid. p. 104. The Bolshevik attitude changed later in the year when, having gained the decisive influence in the trade unions, they sought to subordinate the factory committees to the trade unions.

16

meetings and conferences independently of the Soviet as a whole and its decisions on matters of labour policy were accepted as authoritative by the workers.

AFTER THE OCTOBER REVOLUTION

This multiplicity of overlapping organizations gave rise to much confusion and friction soon after the October revolution. Having assumed power, the Bolsheviks were anxious to bring some order out of the revolutionary chaos. The old machinery of the State had been crushed, and the economy of the country had lost any sign of coherence. Centralization of political power and of economic control was now indispensable if the newly-formed Soviet Government was to survive. At their first attempts at central control over industry, the Bolsheviks came into conflict with the factory committees, on which they had so strongly relied prior to the revolution. The anarchic characteristics of the committees made themselves felt: every factory committee aspired to have the last and final say on all matters affecting the factory, its output, its stock of raw materials, its conditions of work, etc., and paid little or no attention to the needs of industry as a whole. A few weeks after the upheaval, the factory committees attempted to form their own national organization which was to secure their virtual economic dictatorship. The Bolsheviks now called upon the trade unions to render a special service to the nascent Soviet State and to discipline the factory committees. The unions came out firmly against the attempt of the factory committees to form a national organization of their own. They prevented the convocation of a planned All-Russian Congress of factory committees and demanded total subordination on the part of the committees. The committees, however, were too strong to surrender altogether. Towards the end of 1917 a compromise was reached, under which the factory committees accepted a new status: they were to form

17

the primary organizations upon which the trade unions based themselves; but by the same token they were, of course, incorporated in the unions. Gradually they gave up the ambition to act, either locally or nationally, in opposition to the trade unions or independently of them. The unions now became the main channels through which the Government was assuming effective control over industry.

This was roughly the situation when the first All-Russian Congress of the Trade Unions assembled in Moscow in the second week of January 1918.[1] The trade unions had asserted themselves against the factory committees, but in other respects their position had not been clearly defined. Not only did the spokesmen of the various parties—Bolsheviks, Mensheviks, Social Revolutionaries and Anarchists—advance conflicting views; but also within the ranks of Bolshevik trade unionists there was as yet little agreement on the principles of the new trade unionism.

DEBATES AT THE FIRST TRADE UNION CONGRESS

The issue before the Congress was in the words of Mikhail Tomsky, the leading Bolshevik trade unionist, whether 'the trade unions should tie their fortunes to those of the Soviet government or whether they should remain independent organs of economic class struggle?' Tomsky's own answer was clear enough, if only general in character:

Even before the October revolution the general condition of industry compelled the Trade Unions to give up strike action. . . Now, when the proletariat has assumed the political and economic leadership of the country and removed the *bourgeoisie* from the management of industry, the struggle of the workers for the improvement of their position has naturally had to take on new forms, the forms of an organized action, through the Trade Unions and through various regulating bodies, upon the economic

[1] This was the first fully-fledged Trade Union Congress in the whole history of Russia. In 1905 and 1906 and then in the summer of 1917 only conferences of active trade unionists but not of elected delegates took place.

policy of the working class as a whole. The sectional interests of groups of workers have had to be subordinated to the interests of the entire class.[1]

Against this the Mensheviks advocated the independence of the trade unions. Their argument was put briefly by Maisky:

Comrades, although other views are now popular among many workers, we still think that our revolution remains, as we used to say, a bourgeois revolution, and that the Trade Unions have therefore to perform their customary jobs . . . I suppose that capitalism will unfortunately very soon reassert itself with all its might and power. I think therefore that if capitalism remains intact, the tasks with which Trade Unions are confronted under capitalism remain unaltered as well.[2]

This argument was in line with the traditional Menshevik view that the Russian revolution could not, because of Russia's backward and more or less feudal outlook, be socialist in character, and that it could only usher in a bourgeois-democratic republic. What was implied in Maisky's argument was that if, contrary to the Menshevik forecast, the revolution should develop along socialist lines, then there was no reason for socialists to insist on the independence of the trade unions—their task would then be to assist the Government in the transformation of the economic and social system. In appearance at least, there was no difference between the Bolsheviks and the Mensheviks on this crucial point. The role of the trade unions was seen by both to be secondary, and the discussion centred primarily on the prospects of the revolution.

A more sophisticated exposition of the Menshevik view was given at the Congress by Martov, the founder of the school, who also argued that Lenin's experiment in socialism was utopian and bound to collapse. The trade unions, Martov concluded, should not be allowed to be involved in a fore-doomed experiment. To this characteristically Menshevik

---

[1] See Tomsky's Preface to *1. Vserossiiskii Syezd Profsoyuzov.*
[2] *1. Vserossiiskii Syezd Profsoyuzov*, p. 11.

argument Martov added another point not necessarily connected with it: 'In this historic situation this government cannot represent the working class only. It cannot but be a *de
facto* administration connected with a heterogeneous mass of
toiling people, with proletarian and non-proletarian elements
alike. It cannot, therefore, conduct its economic policy along
the lines of consistently and clearly expressed interests of the
working class.'[1] The trade unions, as exponents of the strictly
proletarian interest, should reserve their freedom of action
vis-à-vis the Government. Three years later, Lenin, while
rejecting Martov's general evaluation of the prospects of the
revolution, was to repeat almost literally this part of Martov's
argument. For the time being, however, most Bolsheviks
refused to accept it. Only a few of them, for instance Lozovsky, the future leader of the Red Trade Union International
(Profintern), and Ryazanov had their doubts. They argued
that the socialist development of Russia would be possible
only if socialist revolution won in western Europe as well and
that, failing this, a capitalist restoration in Russia was
probable—it was therefore dangerous for the working class to
curtail the right of coalition: '. . . we, Marxists, should not
conceal from ourselves,' said Ryazanov, 'that as long as the
social revolution begun here has not merged with the social
revolution of Europe and of the whole world . . . the Russian
proletariat . . . must be on its guard and must not renounce
a single one of its weapons . . . it must maintain its Trade
Union organization.'[2] In the light of this argument, too, the
trade unions appeared to retain their usefulness mainly as a
reserve weapon of the workers in case of counter-revolution.
Under a socialist regime their usefulness appeared to be
doubtful.

The practical question, however, with which the Congress
was confronted was not how to provide against the contin-

[1] ibid. p. 80.   [2] ibid. p. 27.

gencies of counter-revolution, but how to find for the trade unions a new place in the revolution. The question which Zinoviev, on behalf of the party, put before the Congress seemed to most delegates to admit one answer only: 'I ask you,' said Zinoviev, 'why and from whom do you need independence: from your own government. . . ? The Trade Unions have already issued decrees on requisitions and on many other measures of prime importance, decrees which are normally issued only by the state administration.'[1]

Thus, at this stage, the official Bolshevik view was that the trade unions should be subordinated to the Government, since they themselves acted as part of the administration. But did this mean that the trade unions should be completely absorbed by the administration, that they should be 'statified'?[2] If so, how were bodies which counted three million members[3] to be fitted in with the machinery of the new State? What was to be their relationship with the Soviets, that backbone of the new republic? Lozovsky described to the Congress the constant friction between Soviets and trade unions that had developed in the few months since the revolution.[4] The Soviets demanded that the trade unions should take their orders from them. The All-Russian Central Council of Trade Unions (ACCTU) protested against this and impressed upon its branches that they did not come under the Soviets and that they should not allow the latter to interfere with the direction of the economic struggle. Although they accepted subordination to the Government as a matter of high policy, the Bolshevik trade unionists jealously guarded the prerogatives of their organization. At the same time the Central Council of the Trade Unions was gaining considerable influence inside the new governmental machine.

[1] ibid. p. 75.
[2] This is a literal translation of the Russian word used throughout this controversy, for which there is no suitable English equivalent.
[3] 1. *Vserossiiskii Syezd Profsoyuzov*, p. 29.　　[4] ibid. p. 31

As Lozovsky told the Congress, ACCTU was, immediately after the revolution, accorded thirty-five seats, from one-fourth to one-third of all seats on the Central Executive Committee of the Soviets, the highest legislative and executive body during the intervals between the All-Russian Congresses of the Soviets.[1] The trade unions were also invited to send their delegates to most of the other newly-formed governmental bodies. ACCTU was often prevented from accepting such invitations by shortage of personnel and it passed on the invitations to the central committees of particular trade unions.

In spite of all this, Lozovsky objected to Zinoviev's description of trade unions as 'organs of governmental power': '. . . the Trade Unions would . . . lose very much. . . What would it mean for them to become "organs of state power"? This would mean that the decisions of the Trade Unions would be carried out by compulsion . . . that they would not be connected with the activity of the mass of productive workers.'[2] Coercion, Lozovsky went on, would take the place of spontaneous class solidarity. Under full socialism the statification of the trade unions would probably be justified, but Russia would become socialist only after the revolution had won in the west, and until then the trade unions should not allow themselves to be absorbed by the State.[3] This division between adherents and opponents of statification cut across normal party divisions: some Left Social Revolutionaries advocated the incorporation of the trade unions by the State more categorically than did the Bolsheviks.[4]

The resolution adopted by the Congress reflected, at least in part, this conflict of views.[5] It rejected political neutrality

---

[1] ibid. p. 35. The Central Executive Committee of the Soviets consisted of 101 members in November 1917, immediately after the revolution. Through co-option and additional elections their number grew to 200 in the course of 1918.

[2] ibid. p. 97.   [3] ibid. p. 197.   [4] ibid. p. 128.   [5] ibid. p. 364 ff.

of the trade unions as a 'bourgeois idea', for 'there is and there can be no neutrality in the great historic struggle between revolutionary socialism and its opponents'. The trade unions pledged their support to the Government in all essential matters:

> The centre of gravity of Trade Union work must now shift to the organizational-economic sphere . . . the Trade Unions ought to shoulder the main burden of organizing production and of rehabilitating the country's shattered productive forces. Their most urgent tasks consist in their energetic participation in all central bodies called upon to regulate output, in the organization of workers' control, registration and redistribution of labour force, organization of exchange between town and countryside, in the most active participation in the demobilization of industry, in the struggle against sabotage and in enforcing the general obligation to work, and so on.

The mere enumeration of these functions showed the trade unions as most important props of the new regime. Yet the Congress of the Trade Unions could not bring itself to declare that the trade unions would at once form part and parcel of the new administration—it spoke about their statification in vague and conditional terms:

> As they develop (v razvernutom vide) the Trade Unions should, in the process of the present socialist revolution, become organs of socialist power, and as such they should work in co-ordination with, and subordination to other bodies in order to carry into effect the new principles. . .
> The Congress is convinced that in consequence of the foreshadowed process, the Trade Unions will inevitably become transformed into organs of the socialist state, and the participation in the Trade Unions will for all people employed in any industry be their duty vis-à-vis the state.

The resolution implied that in the nearest future the trade unions would be hybrid organizations, performing many vital functions for the State, but remaining outside the formal framework of the governmental machine. Two general principles seemed to have been accepted: (a) that in a socialist economy the State would completely incorporate the trade unions, and (b) that socialist economy was not yet in existence and the trade unions still had a role of their own to perform.

But the main specific questions concerning that role were left open. The Congress could not make up its mind, for instance, on whether the unions should continue to resort to strike action in defence of their members. A motion, tabled by Tsyperovich, a prominent Bolshevik trade unionist, which answered the question in the affirmative, was rejected.[1] On the other hand the Bolshevik Party with its fresh memories of its own pre-revolutionary activity was not ready to come out explicitly against strikes.

A number of administrative functions ('State-functions' as Lenin put it) was transferred to the trade unions. A decree issued in December 1917 entrusted the unions with the administration of all social insurance schemes, even though this might as well have been the job of the newly-formed Commissariat of Labour, which it indeed became somewhat later. The Commissariat of Labour and the trade unions overlapped from the beginning, although Schmidt, the head of the Commissariat, was appointed on a proposal of the trade unions and was himself a trade unionist.

The trade unions further formed 'control-distributive commissions' whose task it was to exercise direct and indirect control over industry, through so-called local control commissions elected by workers in the workshops. The control-distributive commissions were half elected by the factory control commissions and half appointed by the trade unions. At that time, we know, the Soviet Government was not yet committed to immediate and wholesale socialization of industry. But privately-owned factories were under workers' control, which, since the relegation of the factory committees, was carried out by the control-distributive commissions of the trade unions. A resolution on this subject stated *inter alia*[2] that 'it was the task of workers' control to put an end to autocracy in the economic field just as an end has been put to it

[1] ibid. p. 367.   [2] ibid. pp. 369–72.

in the political field.' Industrial management by committee as opposed to individual management was still the characteristically revolutionary feature of economic policy.

All forms of economic organization were in utter flux, however; and so the prerogatives of the trade unions could not be clearly defined. More important still, the whole concept of workers' control over industry (with private ownership still tolerated) was soon to be abandoned, under the pressure of civil war; and the trade unions had to adjust themselves to the needs of a new situation.

TRADE UNIONS IN THE CIVIL WAR

When civil war flared up in 1918 the Bolsheviks possessed little more than the rudiments of an administrative machine of their own. The old army had disintegrated and a new one had to be formed. No governmental organization existed capable of recruiting men for the Red Army and of insuring supplies. The Soviets were apparently not solid enough and the party itself was too small in numbers to cope with these tasks. The trade unions, whose nominal membership grew to 3·5 million in the first year of the fighting, transformed themselves into organs of civil war. It was mainly through them that the Government assessed and mobilized manpower. The Central Council of the trade unions issued weekly progress reports on this work, and most trade unions formed special supply services for the Red Army. As the civil war dragged on the trade unions called up and armed 50 per cent of their own members.

The unions assumed an entirely new and enormous responsibility when the Government, afraid that privately-owned industry would not work for the needs of the Red Army, speeded up the process of total socialization, at first as a matter of military rather than of economic policy. Workers' control, in the sense given to it in 1917, came to an

25

end. Unexpectedly for both the Bolshevik Party and the trade unions, the 'State functions' of the latter expanded with enormous rapidity, even though the administration of social insurance, at this stage more nominal than real anyhow, was transferred back from the trade unions to the Commissariat of Labour in December 1918.

In line with this development the second All-Russian Congress of Trade Unions (January 1919) placed more emphasis than did its predecessor on the 'State functions' of unions. The Congress sanctioned the arrangements under which the unions had become at once military recruiting offices, supply services, punitive organs, and so on. Tomsky had no hesitation in stating: 'At this moment when the Trade Unions regulate wages and conditions of labour, when the appointment of the Commissar for Labour, too, depends on our Congress, no strikes can take place in Soviet Russia.'[1] Addressing the Congress, Lenin spoke about the 'inevitable statification of the Trade Unions' and illustrated his point by saying that a Supreme Council of National Economy had just been set up primarily by the trade unions to direct the entire economy of the republic. 'It is not enough to proclaim the dictatorship of the proletariat . . . it is necessary that the Trade Unions merge with the organs of state power and that they take over the entire large scale economic construction. . .' It was possible to argue over the pace of the merger, and Lenin held it to be a mistake to try and effect it 'at a single stroke'. But the general trend of the development was—in Lenin's view—beyond dispute.[2]

It would, nevertheless, be wrong to describe Lenin at this

---

[1] 2. *Vserossiiskii Syezd Profsoyuzov*, p. 96. This change in the trade unions, even though it had been caused by the civil war, did not fail to provoke ferment in the Bolshevik Party. At the second Trade Union Congress, Lozovsky, having left the party, spoke as an independent 'internationalist' against Bolshevik policy in the unions (ibid. p. 37).

[2] ibid. pp. 31–2.

stage as an advocate of statification *tout court*. His view on the new trade unions was part of a wider conception of the Soviet State. He saw the trade unions as being incorporated by the State; but at the same time he kept on expounding his ideas about the 'withering away' of the State. The State was gradually to cease to be a distinct administrative machine separated from, opposed to, and elevated above the people. Every shepherd, 'every cook' was to learn the business of government so that there should be no need for a special body of civil servants. The trade unions were to educate the mass of the workers in the arts of administration. 'We must ever more broaden', these were Lenin's words, 'the participation of the workers themselves in the direction of the economy . . . if we fail to convert the Trade Unions into organs educating the masses, on a scale ten times larger than at present, for the immediate participation in the direction of the state, then we shall not achieve our objective in building communism'.[1]

However, the 'withering away' of the State, for all the doctrinal importance attached to this point, was a matter of the future, whereas the merger of trade unions and the administration was of urgent practical significance. But the implications of the merger were not clear. Were the trade unions to absorb the State or *vice versa*? So far this question had not even been posed: and the two variants of the merger were often confused. Sometimes the claim of the unions to dominate a particular branch of the administration was openly recognized, as in the case of the Commissariat of Labour. At the second Congress of the Trade Unions Schmidt thus described the relationship between his Commissariat and the trade unions:

> The role of the Commissariat . . . should be to give obligatory effect to the recommendations and plans worked out by the Trade Unions.

[1] ibid. p. 33. The same idea was expressed in the debate by Ryazanov: 'But our ideal is not further statification but the de-statification of the entire social life' (ibid. p. 39).

Moreover, not only must the Commissariat not interfere with the prerogatives of the Unions, but even the organs of the Commissariat . . . should,
as far as possible, be formed by the Trade Unions themselves. Here, at
the centre, we act consistently upon this principle. Not only does the All-
Russian Central Council of the Trade Unions propose the candidate for
the post of the People's Commissar for Labour—the Trade Unions have
also organized the entire leading team [Collegium] of the Commissariat.[1]

At this stage already a conflict that was to loom large in
Soviet labour policy began to cast its shadow ahead. The
Supreme Council of National Economy had begun to function. This was the nucleus of the new economic administration, gradually extending its control, through the so-called
Glavki, the managements of national industrial trusts, over
the whole field of industry. The trade unions had to be reorganized so that their vertical structure should correspond
to that of the industrial administration. The apparatus of the
Supreme Council of National Economy was, as we know,
set up in co-operation with the trade unions, but it soon
acquired an identity of its own. More and more often the
trade unions and the Supreme Council of National Economy
(VSNKh) came into conflict. The VSNKh was inclined to
regard the Unions as its auxiliaries, whereas at least some
trade unionists held that the actual direction of industry was
a prerogative of the unions. The conflict was aggravated when
the VSNKh secured the co-operation of a number of technical specialists and old-time economic administrators, upon
whom many trade unionists habitually looked with the
utmost distrust. Here was clearly a great and dramatic conflict in the making.

'POINT FIVE' OF THE 1919 PROGRAMME

An attempt to give a new programmatic definition to the
position of the trade unions was made by the Communist

[1] ibid. p. 47. The Congress adopted a special resolution urging close
co-operation between the provincial branches of the two bodies, for in the
provinces their relations had by no means been smooth.

Party at its eighth Congress, in March 1919, when the party discussed and adopted a new programme.

In its 'Economic Section' (Point 5) the new programme of the party stated:

> The organizational apparatus of socialized industry ought to be based, in the first instance, on the Trade Unions. These ought progressively to free themselves from craft-like narrowness and transform themselves into large associations based on production and embracing the majority of the toilers in any branch of industry. . .
>
> Participating already, in accordance with the laws of the Soviet Republic and established practice, in all local and central organs of industrial administration, *the Trade Unions ought in the end actually to concentrate in their hands all the administration of the entire national economy*. . . The participation of the Trade Unions in economic management . . . constitutes also the chief means of the struggle against the bureaucratization of the economic apparatus. . . (My italics. I. D.)[1]

This paragraph, the famous Point 5 of the Party Programme, was to be invoked in later years by Bolshevik groups advocating the economic supremacy of the trade unions in the Soviet State. 'Point 5' was, in the interpretation of those groups, the Magna Charta of the new trade unionism. And indeed, the view that 'the Trade Unions ought in the end actually to concentrate in their hands all the administration of the entire national economy' savoured of syndicalism, to which the Bolshevik Party, as a whole, had always been opposed. Lenin and the other Bolshevik leaders would soon have to do a lot of explaining away in order to invalidate this promissory note which the party so solemnly and authoritatively handed to the trade unions. In all probability, 'Point 5' was a 'syndicalist' slip committed by the Bolshevik leadership in a mood of genuine gratitude to the trade unions for the work performed by them in the civil war. The 1919 Programme, however, contained also other clauses which may be said to have cancelled out 'Point 5' and limited, at any rate for the immediate future, the prerogatives of the

[1] *V.K.P. (b) o Profsoyuzakh*, p. 95.

trade unions by making labour policy a responsibility of the Soviets as well as of the unions:

Moreover, the Soviet government . . . has established in the Code of Labour Laws . . . the participation of labour organizations in the solution of problems of employment and release of labour. . . [it has established] state-regulated wages on the basis of tariffs worked out by Trade Unions . . . and organs for the assessment and distribution of the labour force, organs which are attached to Soviets and Trade Unions and are obliged to provide work for the unemployed.[1]

Other points of the Programme also dealt with the role of the trade unions. 'Point 6' stated: 'The next task of the economic policy of the Soviet government is . . . maximum utilization of all available labour force, its correct distribution and redistribution as between various geographic areas and various branches of the national economy, a task which [the Soviets] can accomplish only in close co-operation with the Trade Unions.' 'Point 7': 'In view of the disintegration of capitalist organization of labour, the productive forces of the country can be rehabilitated and further developed and the socialist method of production can be enhanced only on the basis of comradely discipline among the toilers and of an utmost expansion of active citizenship [*samodeyatelnost*]. . .' 'The attainment of this objective requires stubborn and systematic work for the re-education of the masses, which has now been made easier because the working masses see that the capitalists, landlords, and merchants have in fact been eliminated. Through their own experience the masses arrive at the conviction that the standard of their well-being depends exclusively on their own disciplined work. In the creation of a new socialist discipline the main role falls to the Trade Unions. Abandoning old clichés . . . the Trade Unions ought to adopt and try out in practice . . . labour accountancy, norms of output, responsibility [of workers] before special comradely workers' courts, etc.'

[1] ibid. p. 102.

In 'Point 8' the Programme urged the unions to impress upon the workers the need to work with, and learn from bourgeois technicians and specialists and to overcome the 'ultra-radical' distrust of the latter. The workers, it was stated, could not build socialism without going through a period of apprenticeship to the bourgeois intelligentsia. On social policy the Programme stated *inter alia*: 'Striving for equality of remuneration for every kind of work, striving for full communism, the Soviet government cannot set itself the task of bringing about that equality now, immediately, when only the first steps are being made in the transition from capitalism to communism.' Payment of high salaries and premiums to bourgeois specialists was therefore sanctioned. This was, according to an expression used by Lenin, the ransom which the young proletarian State had to pay the bourgeois-bred technicians and scientists for services with which it could not dispense. Wages to manual workers, however, were still regulated in a more or less egalitarian spirit.[1]

Although the Programme and many other resolutions tried to clarify the position of the unions, the trade unions, the Supreme Council of National Economy, the Commissariat of Labour, and the multiple organs of the Soviets continued to overlap and clash with one another. The more confused their mutual relations, the more strongly did the Communist Party insist on its own supreme control over all those bodies. This was exercised through the system of party cells inside the trade unions.

The eighth conference of the party (December 1919) worked out a statute which defined rigidly the rights and prerogatives of the cells.[2] The general idea of the statute was not new—it dated back to pre-revolutionary Bolshevik schemes of organization. What was new was the elaborate

[1] ibid. pp. 95–102.　　[2] ibid. pp. 109–10.

detail of the scheme calculated to secure for the party a leading role in every organization. These were the main provisions:

(*a*) Wherever at least three members of the party belonged to a trade union, they were obliged to form a cell (*fraktsya*— fraction) which was to take its orders from the corresponding regional or local party committee outside the trade union.

(*b*) If, inside a trade union, members of the party formed a fairly large group their *fraktsya* elected a bureau which was in charge of the entire party work inside the union.

(*c*) The *fraktsya* enjoyed autonomy *vis-à-vis* the party hierarchy in matters concerning the internal affairs of the *fraktsya*; but in case of a conflict between it and the party committee outside the trade union, the party committee had the last word. The party committee also had unrestricted right of appointment and dismissal: it could send any Communist, even if he was not a member of the trade union, to serve on the Communist *fraktsya* inside the trade union; and it could order any Communist to leave any office in the trade union to which he had been elected.

(*d*) The *fraktsya* proposed its candidates to trade union offices in agreement with the local, regional, or central committee of the party.

(*e*) The *fraktsya*, or its bureau, discussed and took preliminary decisions on every issue which was expected to be placed on the agenda of any trade union body. Communist trade unionists were obliged to vote unanimously at the general meetings of the trade unions in accordance with decisions taken inside the *fraktsya*, but they were free to oppose those decisions during the preliminary discussion inside the *fraktsya*.

This system ran through the entire structure of the trade unions, from factory committee at the bottom to central committees of the trade unions and to the All-Russian Central

Council of the Trade Unions at the top.[1] The Communist trade unionist was thus a Communist first and only then a trade unionist, and by his disciplined behaviour he enabled the party to lead the trade unions.

INDIVIDUAL MANAGEMENT AND LABOUR ARMIES

The ninth Congress of the party (March–April 1920) and the third All-Russian Congress of the Trade Unions (April 1920) marked a new turn. The Bolshevik leaders then hoped that the civil war was at an end and that they would soon be free to turn towards the peaceful reconstruction of Russia's ruined economy. This hope was deferred, for the Russo-Polish war and the campaign against General Wrangel were still ahead. Nevertheless, the ninth Congress of the party sanctioned certain preparations for the transition to peace. The measures adopted were, as later developments showed, not always well suited to smooth that transition. The Bolshevik leaders were not fully aware of the vastness of the devastation and the chaos left behind by the civil war. Nor did they make sufficient allowance for the weariness of the urban working class and the discontent of the peasantry. By inertia they carried on with the system of military communism established during the civil war. The main features of this were: conscription of all available man-power and wealth; socialization of all industrial property; prohibition of private trade; compulsory direction of labour; strict rationing of consumers' goods; payment of wages in kind; and requisitioning of agricultural produce from the peasants (in lieu of taxation). The ninth Congress foreshadowed the continuation and extension of these methods in time of peace. Two new measures stood in the centre of debate: (a) the introduction of individual management in industry in place

[1] This system of cells was built up in every non-party organization, not only in the trade unions.

of management by committee, prevalent hitherto; and (*b*) further militarization of labour and formation of labour armies.

The substitution of individual for collective management in industry met with considerable opposition inside the trade unions, and its actual realization was delayed until 1922. The motive for this reform was economic expediency. Management by committee was found to be inefficient; the need for greater industrial discipline had become painfully obvious; and greater efficiency could be secured by individual management. It is enough to recall that only recently the trade unions had proclaimed an end to 'economic autocracy in industry' to understand why the return to individual management could not but be decried by many trade unionists as the reappearance of that autocracy, even though the present managers were not the old industrialists or their nominees but directors appointed by the proletarian State. The authoritative spokesmen of the party—Lenin, Trotsky, and Bukharin—met the objections to individual management with the argument that the standing of the working class, as the ruling class in the Soviet Republic, was not involved in this controversy over individual or collective management. The working class, they stated, would through its representative organs merely delegate its power of economic disposition to industrial managers: 'Individual management does not in any degree limit or infringe upon the rights of the [working] class or the "rights" of the Trade Unions, because the class can exercise its rule in one form or another, as technical expediency may dictate. It is the ruling class at large which in every case "appoints" persons for the managerial and administrative jobs'.[1]

A resolution submitted by Trotsky and adopted by the

[1] *V.K.P. (b) o Profsoyuzakh*, p. 128.

34

Congress of the party did in fact allow the trade unions to exercise a very strong influence upon the appointment of industrial managers. The organization of industrial management 'should be carried out by agreement between the organs of the Supreme Council of National Economy and the corresponding organs of the Central Council of the Trade Unions.'[1]

Four types of industrial management were provided for:

(a) Intelligent and energetic trade unionists might be appointed to posts of industrial managers. This was the most favoured variant, but the difficulty was that not many trade unionists with managerial abilities were available.

(b) Bourgeois technicians or specialists might be appointed to managerial posts. A manager of this category was supervised by a trade unionist commissar, in the same way in which the military specialist in the Army was supervised by the political commissar, who could veto his orders.

(c) Alternatively, a bourgeois technician could be appointed as manager with two trade unionists as assistant managers, who could, however, exercise no veto over his decisions. (This was apparently the case when the bourgeois technician was beyond suspicion of hostility towards the Soviet regime.)

(d) Management by committee was left in existence if the work of the managerial team had been satisfactory, but even then the powers of the chairman of the team were extended.

Meanwhile it was the task of the trade unions to train their advanced members for managerial responsibilities. Special trade union training centres were set up for this purpose.

The labour armies represented a more fundamental issue of economic and labour policy affecting the trade unions. The originator of the labour armies was Trotsky, but at that time (1920) his scheme had the backing of the entire party leader-

[1] ibid. p. 117.

ship.[1] It arose empirically, in connexion with the planned demobilization of the Red Army. Towards the end of the civil war transport was completely paralysed, because of the destruction of rolling-stock and railway lines. It was impossible to release the soldiers and send them home. Entire divisions and armies wasted their time in inactivity, while industrial and in part agricultural production were at a standstill. It was then decided to employ idle detachments in coal-mining, timber-felling, harvesting, etc. Later the Government proceeded to mobilize civilian labour as well—it was only a step from the employment of armed forces as labour battalions to the organization of civilian labour into military units. In the aftermath of the civil war, amid its appalling misery and complete breakdown of labour discipline, the Government hoped to break in this way what looked like a hopeless economic deadlock.[2]

At the third Congress of the Trade Unions Trotsky defended the labour armies. His most vocal, though not the only, critics were the Mensheviks, who still enjoyed some freedom of expression and argued that militarization of labour would lower and not raise productivity, for high productivity could be obtained with free labour only. The central point in Trotsky's counter-argument was the denial of any real difference between voluntary and compulsory labour:

Let the Menshevik speakers explain to us [these were Trotsky's words] what is meant by free, non-compulsory labour? We have known slave-

[1] In later years it became the fashion to decry the labour armies and to suggest that Trotsky exclusively was responsible for them. Yet Stalin himself served as the chairman of the Ukrainian Council of the Labour Army, while Trotsky, as chairman of the Council of Labour and Defence, headed the all-Russian organization.

[2] In his report to the third Congress of the Trade Unions, Rykov, then chief of the Supreme Council of National Economy, stated that because of lack of fuel not a single furnace was in operation in the entire Donetz Basin. The output of the Donetz coal mines was only about 300,000 tons a month, about 10 per cent of pre-war. The entire output of the steel industry was less than 5 per cent of pre-war. Only 6 per cent of all textile spindles were in operation. (*3. Vserossiiskii Syezd Profsoyuzov*, p. 80.)

labour, serf-labour, compulsory regimented labour in the medieval crafts, and the labour of free wage-earners which the *bourgeoisie* calls free labour. We are now heading towards the type of labour that is socially regulated on the basis of an economic plan, obligatory for the whole country, compulsory for every worker. This is the basis of socialism. . . The militarization of labour, in this fundamental meaning of which I have spoken, is the indispensable, basic method for the organization of our labour forces. . . If our new form of organization of labour were to result in lower productivity, then, *ipso facto*, we would be heading for disaster. . . But is it true that compulsory labour is always unproductive? . . . This is the most wretched and miserable liberal prejudice: chattel-slavery, too, was productive. Its productivity was higher than that of slave-labour, and in so far as serfdom and feudal lordship guaranteed the security of the towns . . . and of peasant labour, in so far it was a progressive form of labour. Compulsory serf-labour did not grow out of the feudal lords' ill-will. It was a progressive phenomenon. . . The whole history of mankind is the history of its education for work, for higher productivity of labour. This is by no means so simple a task, for man is lazy and he has the right to be so. . . Even free wage-labour was not productive at first . . . it became so gradually after a process of social education. All sorts of methods were used for that education. The *bourgeoisie* at first drove the peasant out to the high roads and grabbed his land. When the peasant refused to work in the factories, the *bourgeoisie* branded him with hot iron, hanged, or shot him and so forcibly trained him for manufacture. . . Our task is to educate the working class on socialist principles. What are our methods for that?

They are not less varied than those used by the *bourgeoisie*, but they are more honest, more direct and frank, uncorrupted by mendacity and fraud. The *bourgeoisie* had to pretend that its system of labour was free, and it deceived the simple-minded about the productivity of that labour. We know that every labour is socially compulsory labour. Man must work in order not to die. He does not want to work. But the social organization compels and whips him into that direction. The new, socialist order differs from the bourgeois one in that with us labour is performed in the interest of society, and therefore we need no priestly, church-like, liberal or Menshevik recipes for raising the labour energy of the proletariat. . . The first way of disciplining and organizing labour is to make the economic plan clear to the widest masses of the toilers. When we transfer a worker from one spot to another, when we call up the peasant for labour duty, those called up should first of all be convinced that they are not being called up for nothing, that those who have mobilized them have a definite plan, that a necessary economic job must be performed at the spot where the labour force has now been placed. . .

37

Wages, under present conditions, must not be viewed from the angle of securing the personal existence of the individual worker; they should above all serve to evaluate what that individual worker contributes to the workers' republic. Wages should measure the conscientiousness, usefulness, and efficiency of the work of every labourer. As long as we are poor, as long as we do not have enough food to satisfy minimum needs, we cannot distribute it equally to all workers, and we shall allocate consumers' goods . . . to essential workers. . . We are obliged to act in this way for the sake of the country's future and in order to save the working masses.[1]

This is, as far as we know, the frankest statement of what may conditionally be termed a totalitarian labour policy, perhaps the only attempt at a sociological and philosophical justification of such a policy that has ever been made in Russia or elsewhere. Trotsky proclaimed the unrestricted right of the proletarian State to use the labour power of the nation in the way it considered proper and the duty of the trade unions to concern themselves with the worker as a producer and not as a consumer. The trade unions ought to discipline the worker, to raise his efficiency, to get him interested in the management and organization of industry rather than to defend his claims to higher wages and better working conditions. All these would no doubt become available with the growth of the national income earned by the socialized economy, and therefore the trade unions should preoccupy themselves with the *national* income rather than with the *individual* incomes of the workers. In view of all this—such was Trotsky's as yet unspoken conclusion—the trade unions, in their old form, had played out their role. As producers' organizations they would have little in common with the old trade unions, except the name.

In making his striking statements, Trotsky elevated an expedient to a principle, and, as so often happens, made an ideological virtue out of a bitter necessity. His immediate purpose was to justify the labour armies and to prove the inescapable need for them; but he could have easily done this

[1] *3. Vserossiiskii Syezd Profsoyuzov*, pp. 87, 96.

on the ground that the labour armies were a desperate emergency measure, without necessarily proclaiming the unlimited right of the State permanently to conscript labour and without declaring militarization of labour to be of the essence of socialist planning. In later years Trotsky himself became the strongest critic of a labour policy of which he had unwittingly been an inspirer. Trotsky's philosophy of labour came to underlie Stalin's practical labour policy in the thirties, although Stalin and his adherents would for obvious reasons (and for one special reason to be discussed later) never admit it. Moreover, in Stalin's practice Trotsky's theory was not only embodied, but also exaggerated and brutalized *ad absurdum*.

From a Marxist viewpoint, Trotsky's argument contained a half-truth only. Marxist economic theory, like any other sociological theory, does in fact stress the social necessity of labour. 'Man must work in order not to die' remains true under any social system. In this broad sense it is, of course, true that all labour is compulsory. But here the real problem only begins. Marx and his followers devoted their main attention to the differences of form which this compulsion of labour took under different social systems; and to these 'differences of form' they attached the greatest importance. In a society based on slave or serf labour the compulsion was direct, legal, and political. It manifested itself in a social relationship under which the producer himself and/or his product or part of his product were owned by the slave-owner or the feudal lord. In the capitalist order the compulsion became indirect and purely economic. The wage-earner is legally and politically free. He *must* sell his labour power because, unlike the artisan or the peasant, he does not own his means of production, and because he must earn his living. Marx, bitterly as he criticized the capitalist order, repeatedly stressed the 'progressive' implications of this change from direct to indirect compulsion. That labour is free under capitalism is an illusion, but that illusion (and the modern worker's 'formal' freedom on which it is based) has nevertheless heightened the self-confidence of the worker and helped to develop his mental faculties and human dignity. Without it the growth of modern industry and the consequent struggle of the working classes for socialism would hardly have been possible.[1] All Marxists, including the Bolshevik leaders, had hitherto taken it for granted that in comparison with capitalism socialism would ease, and not aggravate, the compulsion of labour and that it would thereby powerfully stimulate its productivity. What Trotsky now dismissed as a 'wretched and miserable liberal prejudice'—the view that compulsory labour was relatively unproductive—belonged in fact to the essence of Marxism. His statement—one of the exaggerations and over-simplifications of military communism —reflected no doubt the strains and stresses of the civil war; but it also suggested a continuation of the methods of war communism into peace.[2]

[1] In a famous footnote to *Capital* Marx wrote: 'This is one of the circumstances that makes production by slave labour such a costly process. The labourer here is, to use a striking expression of the ancients, distinguishable only as *instrumentum vocale*, from an animal as *instrumentum semi vocale*, and from an implement as *instrumentum mutum*. But he himself takes care to let both beast and implement feel that he is none of them, but is a man. He convinces himself with immense satisfaction that he is a different being, by treating the one unmercifully and damaging the other *con amore*. Hence the principle, universally applied in this method of production, only to employ the rudest and heaviest implements and such as are difficult to damage owing to their sheer clumsiness. In the slave states bordering on the Gulf of Mexico, down to the date of the civil war, ploughs constructed on old Chinese models, which turned up the soil like a hog or a mole, instead of making furrows, were alone to be found.'

[2] Trotsky, however, was justified in claiming that he had urged the Politbureau to end military communism as early as February 1920 but that his advice had been rejected. He revealed this at the tenth Congress in the presence of Lenin and other Bolshevik leaders, without being contradicted (*10. Syezd R.K.P. (b)*, pp. 191–2). Since it had been decided to continue with military communism, militarization of labour was inescapable; and Trotsky drew the conclusions of a decision taken against his advice.

Throughout 1920 the trade unions were in a ferment. Opposition groups appeared at almost every level of the organization. In the latter part of the year, after the conclusion of the Russo-Polish war, the repressed discontent broke into the open. The trade unions reacted against the interference of the party in their affairs, and they protested against the appointment and dismissal of trade union officials by the party. The All-Russian Central Council of the Trade Unions split into two factions: one acted on the principle enunciated by Trotsky that the trade unions should view their tasks in the 'productionist' and not 'consumptionist' spirit, while the other faction, headed by Tomsky, insisted on the need for the trade unions to resume, in some measure, the defence of the interests of their members. In this conflict the Politbureau repeatedly intervened, first in favour of Trotsky (August 1920), then against him, until in November he was forbidden to debate the issue in public.[1]

The *cause célèbre* in this controversy was the *Tsektran* or the Central Committee of Transport. This body, headed by Trotsky, was formed at a time when the Russian railways had practically ceased to function, and its task was to revive the transport system. Endowed with wide emergency powers, Trotsky dismissed the leadership of the trade union of railwaymen, proclaimed a state of emergency in transport, militarized labour, and rapidly brought the railways into some working order. The feat was hailed, but Trotsky, carried away by his success, intimated that a 'shake-up' in other trade unions, similar to that which had taken place in the railwaymen's union, was needed, to replace 'irresponsible agitators' by production-minded trade unionists.[2] This brought the trade unions to their feet and at the fifth trade union conference (November 1920) Tomsky openly attacked Trotsky.

[1] *10. Syezd R.K.P. (b)*, pp. 214–15.   [2] ibid. p. 214.

The Central Committee of the party, to which the dispute was referred, was itself divided on the issue. A resolution on the *Tsektran* adopted at a plenary session of the Central Committee was in part a rebuff to Trotsky. It ordered the disbandment of the so-called political departments in transport and called for the democratization of the trade unions and for a stop to the practice of appointing from above officials who should be democratically elected to their posts. But on other essential points the Central Committee backed Trotsky: 'The party ought to educate and support . . . a new type of Trade Unionist, the energetic and imaginative economic organizer who will approach economic issues not from the angle of distribution and consumption but from that of expanding production, who will view them not with the eyes of somebody accustomed to confront the Soviet government with demands and to bargain, but with the eyes of the true economic organizer.'[1]

However, the debates in the Central Committee revealed so profound and many-sided a division of opinion among the Bolshevik chiefs that it was decided to put the whole matter to public debate. Extremely turbulent and confused, the debate lasted throughout the whole winter of 1920–1; it culminated in the tenth Congress of the party (March 1921), one of the most dramatic assemblies in the history of Bolshevism.

THE TRADE UNION CONTROVERSY AT THE TENTH PARTY CONGRESS

In the course of the pre-Congress discussion a great number of factions and groups emerged, each with its own views and 'theses' on trade unions. The differences between some of those groups were very subtle indeed, and nearly all groups referred to so many common principles that sometimes the

[1] Quoted from G. Zinoviev, *Sochinenia* (Moscow, 1924–6), VI, 599–600.

object of the debate seemed almost unreal. However, as the controversy unfolded various groups merged with one another, and in the end only three resolutions were put before the Congress. One motion, put forward by Trotsky and Bukharin, urged the complete 'statification' of the trade unions. A motion emanating from the so-called Workers' Opposition (its leader was the former Commissar of Labour, A. Shlyapnikov) demanded the transfer of the entire economic administration to the trade unions. These were the two extreme attitudes. Lenin, backed by nine other members of the Central Committee, tried to strike a balance between the extremes—his set of resolutions was commonly referred to as the 'Platform of the Ten'.

(a) *The Views of Trotsky–Bukharin.* Trotsky now drew the logical conclusion from the statement on labour policy he had made at the third Congress of the Trade Unions[1]: 'The transformation of the Trade Unions into Production Unions—not only in name but in content and method of work as well—forms the greatest task of our epoch.'[2] The educational work of the trade unions—Trotsky's motion went on—should be focused on the participation of the workers in organizing industry. Their struggle for better living conditions ought to be carried more and more into the sphere of economic organization, and should be directed, for instance, towards raising the productivity of consumers' industries. '. . . the Union ought to embrace all workers . . . from the unskilled ones to the most

---

[1] The 'Trotskyist' motion was signed by the following members of the Central Committee: Trotsky, Bukharin, Andreev, Dzerzhinsky, Krestinsky, Preobrazhensky, Rakovsky, Serebriakov. Among prominent Bolsheviks who backed it were Pyatakov, F. Kon, Larin, and Sokolnikov. In the motion submitted to the Congress Trotsky's view appeared in a diluted form. In the pre-Congress discussion he had urged full and immediate statification of the trade unions, but then he softened his attitude, in part under the influence of Lenin's severe criticism and in order to facilitate coalition with Bukharin's so-called 'buffer group', which had taken an intermediate position between Lenin and Trotsky.

[2] *10. Syezd R.K.P (b)*, p. 454.

qualified technicians, all subordinated to the regime of the proletarian class organization. The Union ought permanently to assess its membership from the angle of production and it should always possess a full and precise characterization of the productive value of any worker. . .'[1] It is necessary that the working masses be fully aware that their interests are best defended by those who raise the productivity of labour, rehabilitate the economy and increase the volume of material goods available. It was from this viewpoint, too, that the election of the leading bodies of the trade unions should be organized.

Trotsky's motion further asserted that:

(a) the statification of the trade unions had in actual fact already been carried very far;

(b) the workers' share in organizing the national economy was insufficient;

(c) the gradual transfer of the economic administration to the trade unions, which the party programme of 1919 had promised, presupposed 'the planned transformation of the Unions into apparatuses of the workers' state'. This, however, was to be achieved gradually, and not by a single juridical act. For the present, it was proposed that the trade unions and the economic administration should be overhauled so that their leading bodies, the Praesidiums of the Central Council of the Trade Unions and of the Supreme Council of National Economy, should have between one-third and

---

[1] The Trotskyist motion, of course, presupposed compulsory membership of trade unions, which had actually been in force throughout the period of military communism. In practice, the workers and employees of a factory 'collectively' adhered to a union, and the individual worker or employee had no right to secede. This explained the phenomenal growth of the trade union membership during the civil war. According to figures given by Zinoviev at the tenth Congress the membership was 1·5 million in July 1917, 2·6 in January 1918, 3·5 in 1919, 4·3 in 1920 and 7 million in 1921. Another reason for this expansion in membership was the inclusion in the trade unions of all employees, civil servants, and professional men who had not been organized before the revolution (ibid. pp, 187–8).

one-half of their members in common. This was to put an end to the 'alienation' or antagonism between the trade unions and the economic administration, an 'alienation' on which Trotsky's motion dwelt with considerable emphasis. The Central Council of the Trade Unions and the Supreme Council of National Economy were to hold joint sessions periodically. Personal union was also to be established between the two organizations in their lower grades. No doubt was left, however, that the trade unions should be subordinate to the economic administration, although it was proposed that they alone should be in charge of distribution and protection of labour and of regulation of wages and working conditions. The Commissariat of Labour, hitherto in charge of those matters, was to be disbanded altogether. It was further proposed that the unions should settle conflicts between the economic administration and the workers, acting as a sort of an arbitration body directly responsible to the Government.

Finally, the position of industrial managers was at least in part to be determined by their standing with the trade unions. Bourgeois technicians and administrators who had become full members of a union were to be entitled to hold managerial posts, without supervision by commissars; those who were only candidates to trade union membership could hold managerial posts but were to be supervised by commissars; and, lastly, politically unreliable persons could serve only as assistant managers on probation.

The wages policy of the statified trade unions should be guided by two principles: (a) shock competition (*udarni-chestvo*) between workers at production; and (b) the levelling out of wages, at least in so far that premiums for high output should be paid out only after a real minimum wage had been secured to all workers. In this respect Trotsky had shifted his ground since the third Congress of the Trade Unions,

45

where he had more emphatically favoured differentiation of wages.

(*b*) *The Workers' Opposition.* The motion of the Workers' Opposition was labelled by its opponents as syndicalist or anarcho-syndicalist. Explicitly or implicitly, it postulated the domination of the trade unions over the State, the abolition of the normal economic administration, and its substitution by the trade unions.

The Workers' Opposition referred, of course, to 'Point 5' of the 1919 programme and charged the leadership of the party with violating its pledges towards the trade unions. 'In practice the leadership of the party and the governmental bodies have in the last two years systematically narrowed the scope of Trade Union work and reduced almost to nil the influence of the working class associations in the Soviet state.'[1] The participation of the trade unions in industrial management meant in practice that the unions were used by the economic administration as reference bureaux or advisory bodies. Conflicts between trade unions, party committees, and the economic authorities had dangerously piled up; and —the Workers' Opposition claimed—the party and the economic authorities, having been swamped by bourgeois technicians and other non-proletarian elements, displayed outright hostility towards the trade unions, a hostility which reflected 'bourgeois class hatred of the proletariat'.

The remedy for all these evils was 'the concentration of industrial management in the hands of the Trade Unions'. The transition to the new system should begin from the lowest industrial unit and extend upwards. At the factory level the factory committee should regain the dominant position it had had at the beginning of the revolution.[2] This demand, it will be remembered, had been raised by anarcho-syndicalist elements in 1917, when it was bitterly opposed by

[1] *10. Syezd R.K.P.* (*b*), p. 360. [2] ibid. pp. 361–2.

46

the Bolshevik-led trade unions. To some extent, therefore, both Lenin and Trotsky were justified in describing the attitude of the Workers' Opposition as anarcho-syndicalist.

The Workers' Opposition proposed the following specific measures: the nominal parity of representation of trade unions and of the economic administration in various controlling bodies should be abolished in favour of predominantly trade union control. 'Not a single person is to be appointed to any administrative-economic post without the agreement of the Trade Unions.' Candidatures proposed by the latter should be binding on the economic authorities. Officials recommended by the trade unions were to remain accountable for their conduct to the unions, who should also have the right to recall them from their posts at any time. This programme culminated in the demand that an 'All-Russian Producers' Congress' be convened to elect the central management of the entire national economy. National congresses of separate trade unions were similarly to elect managements for the various branches of the economy. Local and regional managements should be formed by local trade union conferences, while the management of single factories was to belong to the factory committees which were to remain part of the trade union organization.

Last but not least, the Workers' Opposition proposed a radical revision of the wages policy in an extremely egalitarian spirit: money wages were to be progressively replaced by rewards in kind; the basic food ration was to be made available to workers without any payment; the same was to apply to meals in factory canteens, essential travelling facilities, and facilities for education and leisure, lodging, lighting, etc. No attempt was made to explain how this programme of full communism, theoretically designed for an economy of great plenty, was to be made to work amid the utter poverty of Russian society after the civil war. The only specific

47

palliative suggested was that factories should run their own auxiliary farms to secure the supply of food to their workers.[1]

(c) '*Platform of Ten*'. The motion tabled by Lenin was the most elaborate and carefully balanced of all the resolutions placed before the Congress. Its polemical edge was directed primarily against the Workers' Opposition and only in the second instance against Trotsky—both Lenin and Trotsky made a common front against the Workers' Opposition. The Leninist motion began with a verbal reaffirmation of the principles embodied in 'Point 5' of the 1919 programme, promising the transfer of all economic administration to the trade unions. 'The present situation', the motion went on, 'urgently requires that the Trade Unions should take a more direct part in the organization of production not only through detailing their members to work in the economic administration but through the whole of their own machinery as well.' But, apart from this, the whole tenor of the motion suggested the need for the strictest subordination of trade union policy to the Government. Nevertheless, the idea about the statification of the trade unions was described as erroneous on the ground that statification would not help to improve Russia's economic position and that trade unions absorbed by the State would not be able to perform their proper functions.[2]

What were these functions? The trade unions were to provide a broad *social* base for the proletarian dictatorship exercised by the party. The need for that base was dictated by the peasant character of the country. The ruling class, the

[1] Before the Congress another opposition group, the so-called Group of Democratic Centralism or *Decemists* (Bubnov, Sapronov, Ossinsky, and others), advocated similar views. At the Congress, however, the *Decemists* withdrew their 'Theses' and stated that they would not take part in the 'shadow-boxing' over the trade unions, for the real problem was how to bring the party back to democratic ways. Compared with this the position of the trade unions was a secondary issue.

[2] *V.K.P.* (*b*) *v Rezolutsiyakh*, I, 381.

proletariat, was in a minority, which had to be effectively organized in order to be able to keep under steady political influence the vast peasant majority. The trade unions were, or should be, the broadest voluntary organization of industrial workers. Absorbed by the State they would become a mere bureaucratic machine. The trade unions were further to be the 'school of communism' for their seven million members. Again and again it was pointed out that the Communist Party had only half a million people in its ranks, a minority within the proletarian minority. The Communists must not attempt to impose themselves as the Government's nominees upon the trade unions. Instead they should strive to be accepted by the mass of the trade unionists as its leaders on the strength of their merits and qualities of leadership. Only then could they hope to turn the trade unions into schools of communism for the entire working class.

Trotsky had insisted that the militarization of labour was in the long run essential for the socialist reorganization of economy. Against this the Leninist motion stressed that militarization could not be regarded as a permanent feature of socialist labour policy. The proletarian dictatorship must use persuasion as well as coercion, and it ought carefully to balance the one against the other. Coercion was peculiar to the State, even though the State, too, must, wherever possible, try to attain its ends by persuasion. As a social organization, distinct from the State, the trade unions were in their real element when they worked through persuasion, even though in exceptional cases they, too, might use coercion. It was normal for the State to appoint officials from above. 'The reorganization of the Trade Unions from above would be utterly inexpedient. The methods of a workers' democracy, severely curtailed in the three years of the most savage civil war, ought to be re-established, in the first instance and on the widest possible scale, in the Trade Union movement. It is

49

necessary that the leading bodies of the Trade Unions should in actual fact be elected and broadly based. . .' The methods of coercion and command which had been used to such salutary effect in the Red Army during the civil war must not be extended to the field of economic policy.[1]

A similar balance ought to be struck between the productionist and the consumptionist viewpoints. The trade unions were to take part in the working out of economic plans; they were to propose candidates for administrative-economic jobs, although their proposals were to have the strength of recommendations only; they were to inspect, through specialized departments, the work of the economic administration, to keep account of industrial man-power and its distribution; they were to work out norms of output, this being their exclusive prerogative. 'In view of the fact that the working out of norms of labour . . . has been concentrated in the Trade Unions . . . and that the protection of labour . . . ought to be entirely transferred to the Trade Unions, the Congress considers it necessary that the departments for wage-rate fixing and protection of labour attached hitherto to the Commissariat of Labour . . . should be wound up and transferred to the All-Russian Central Council of Trade Unions.'[2] As

---

[1] ibid. The Leninist motion enumerated the tasks of the trade unions as follows:
(1) To study systematically the work of the economic administration. (2) To exercise functions of control and inspection. (3) To participate in the working out of economic plans and production programmes and in the fixing of economic priorities. (4) To study labour processes from the technical angle. (5) To take part in building up the machinery of economic administration. (6) To watch closely over the assessment and distribution of the manual labour force and technical skill and over the correct utilization of raw materials and fuels. (7) To work out ways and means of combating infringements of labour discipline. (8) To analyse the accumulating technical experience which should be communicated and exchanged at meetings of workers' delegates, in factory committees, etc., with the purpose of immediate utilization of that experience by the economic administration.
The trade unions were to form specialized economic departments to deal with those matters. [2] *V.K.P. (b) v Rezolutsiyakh*, 1, 385.

'schools of labour discipline' the trade unions were to establish 'comradely' disciplinary courts for trying offenders in open session. In addition, trade union 'plenipotentiaries' were to supervise labour discipline in the factories and to supply daily reports to the trade unions.

The motion concluded with a proposal for an overhaul of the trade unions and the economic administration. At the time of the Congress there existed twenty-three national trade unions which had replaced a much greater number of organizations in the previous period. A further reduction of the number of the national trade unions was envisaged, although it was admitted that this would have its disadvantages: while craft sectionalism had been overcome in the trade unions as they merged, every union had now to deal with many more economic authorities than before. The economic administration was therefore to be reorganized so that its structure should correspond to that of the trade unions.

As regards wages, the Leninist motion, too, declared the levelling of wages to be the ultimate objective, but more emphatically than the Trotskyist motion it rejected the extreme egalitarianism of the Workers' Opposition. Wages policy was to be designed so as to 'discipline labour and increase its productivity'. Workers' emulation for higher output, so Lenin argued against Trotsky, could not be squared with equality in consumption. Since wages were paid in kind as well as in money, this implied the need for a differential rationing system to be worked out and put into effect by the joint efforts of the trade unions, the food offices, and the industrial managements.

These then were the three motions that competed for acceptance by the tenth Congress of the party. A comparison between these motions tends up to a point to obscure rather than throw into relief the issue with which the Congress tried to come to grips, because, for tactical reasons, the authors of every motion incorporated passages from their opponents' motions and thereby blurred the real differences. Nor did the Congress try to solve the problem of the trade unions only—the entire structure of the Soviet regime was at stake in this debate.

PROLETARIAN DICTATORSHIP, PROLETARIAN DEMOCRACY, AND TRADE UNIONS

The complete ruin of the Russian industry and the virtual dispersal of the industrial working class formed the background to this controversy. At the fourth Congress of the Trade Unions (May 1921) Miliutin, *rapporteur* of the Supreme Council of National Economy, stated that the output of metal was only 4 per cent of pre-war, while the volume of consumers' goods was only 30 per cent. The cities were depopulated, Petersburg having less than three-quarters of a million inhabitants and Moscow only slightly more than a million. The industrial workers were fleeing from the town into the countryside; those who stayed behind produced very little and spent most of their time trading on the black markets.[1] The disorganization of the entire economy and the demoralization of the working class were further illustrated by statements, made at the fourth Congress of the Trade Unions, that workers in factories were stealing 50 per cent of the goods produced and that the average worker could pay with his wage only one-fifth of his cost of living, being compelled to earn the rest by illicit trading.[2] Bukharin, addressing the Congress on behalf of the party, stated: 'The fundamental danger which now confronts us is that chaos is washing away the strength of the proletariat as a class in action. . . If this class becomes demoralized and hollowed out from inside, the problem is really very grave. . . The workers become petty traders.'[3] In the days of the tenth

[1] *4. Syezd Profsoyuzov*, pp. 72–7. [2] ibid. p. 119. [3] ibid. p. 22.

Congress of the party, popular discontent flared up in the armed risings of Kronstadt, Tambov, and other places in which disillusioned Bolsheviks as well as anti-Bolsheviks took part. For the first time the Bolshevik regime, having emerged triumphantly from the civil war, was really isolated, lacking support from the mass of the people.

Hitherto the entire Bolshevik conception of the Soviet regime and of the place of the trade unions in it had been based on the premiss that at least the industrial working class stood solidly behind the revolution and would continue to do so. Now, three and a half years after the October revolution, this premiss was disproved by the facts. The crisis which ensued was reflected in the trade union debate. Hitherto the Bolshevik Party had taken it for granted that proletarian dictatorship and proletarian democracy (as distinct from formal or bourgeois democracy), far from contradicting one another, were identical, or at least complementary: the dictatorship was suppressing the resistance of landlords and capitalists, but it was based on freedom of expression inside the working classes. Now a conflict arose between proletarian dictatorship and proletarian democracy. In the trade unions, that broadest mass organization of the proletariat, this was felt most acutely. The Workers' Opposition willynilly was the mouthpiece of that same popular discontent that had led even Bolsheviks to join in the Kronstadt rising. The emergence of that opposition inside the ruling party was itself a measure of the social disorganization in the background. It represented a revolt inside the trade unions against dictation by the party and by the economic administration. In quasi-anarchist fashion it evoked the principle of proletarian democracy against the dictatorship.

Most Bolshevik leaders were dimly aware of the symptomatic significance of the Workers' Opposition. But they held that the Opposition expressed the demoralization of the

53

working class, the psychology of the working man turned into the black marketeer and incapable of any constructive attitude towards the new State. They were determined to maintain the proletarian dictatorship, of which they considered the Bolshevik Party to be the trustee, even though for the moment it lacked the democratic support of the proletariat; and they hoped that with economic recovery and political stabilization the dictatorship would be able to base itself once again on proletarian democracy.

This then was the issue which underlay the controversy over the trade unions. The Workers' Opposition argued in fact against the dictatorship of the party when it demanded that the entire management of the national economy be transferred to an All-Russian Congress of Producers. 'We ought to shift,' so Shlyapnikov, the leader of the Opposition, stated, 'the centre of our attention to the factories and workshops. There we ought to start with the organization of our economy. . . At present communists are thrown out of the factory committees. The basis of our Trade Unions, the factory committees, acquire a non-party outlook because the rights that we [the party] leave to our Trade Unions and party cells are negligible.'[1] The spokesmen of the opposition blamed both Lenin and Trotsky as 'economic militarizers' and complained that for all their differences of views they had in fact made common cause against the opposition and the proletarian rank and file. On the other side, Zinoviev, who throughout these debates acted as Lenin's mouthpiece, used the following significant argument against the demand for a Producers' Congress: 'At this Producers' Congress which you want to be convened at this great moment [Zinoviev was referring to the Kronstadt rising still in progress] the majority will consist of non-party people. A good many of them will be Social Revolutionaries and Mensheviks. Should we hand over

[1] *10. Syezd R.K.P. (b)*, pp. 213–14.

54

everything to them? To whom is it not clear that to put the question thus would be to stake the head of the entire proletarian movement?"[1] Trotsky put the issue with even greater bluntness:

The Workers' Opposition has come out with dangerous slogans, making a fetish of democratic principles. They place the workers' right to elect their representatives—above the party, as it were, as if the party were not entitled to assert its dictatorship even if that dictatorship temporarily clashed with the passing moods of the workers' democracy.

It is necessary to create among us the awareness of the revolutionary historical birthright of the party, which is obliged to maintain its dictatorship, regardless of temporary wavering in the spontaneous moods of the masses, regardless of the temporary waverings even in the working classes. This awareness is for us the indispensable unifying element. The dictatorship does not base itself at every given moment on the formal principle of a workers' democracy, although the workers' democracy is, of course, the only method by which the masses can be drawn more and more into political life.

When I argued that workers' democracy should be subordinated to the criterion of the economic interest of the working class. . . Comrade Kamenev stated that in Trotsky's eyes workers' democracy is a conditional proposition. Of course it is, although it is not a conditional but a conditioned proposition. If we were to assume that workers' democracy is unconditional, that it is above everything else, then Comrade Shlyapnikov would have been right when, in his first draft, he stated that every factory should elect its own management, that every district conference of producers should elect its leading bodies, and so forth up to the All-Russian Producers' Congress.[2]

In conclusion Trotsky suggested that the party should, for the time being, cease to advocate and practise proletarian democracy, and that instead it should concentrate on building up a 'producers' democracy'. A regime based on publicly-owned industry, producing not for profit but for the satisfaction of social needs, was by definition proletarian, even though the working class was temporarily in virtual opposition to it. That regime represented the general interest of the proletariat, as distinct from sectional or temporary benefits.

[1] ibid. p. 190.   [2] ibid. p. 192.

The State (or the party) had therefore the right to impose its policies upon the working class. This determined the attitude of the party towards the trade unions. The latter ought to be made to serve the workers' State; they were not entitled to confront that State with traditional claims and demands.

At this point begins the real difference between Trotsky and Lenin. Taking up an argument which had first been advanced by the Menshevik Martov in 1918, Lenin now dismissed as a false syllogism the view that the trade unions had nothing to defend against the workers' State. The Soviet State of the day, he said, was not a workers' State. It was a State of workers and peasants; and in addition it had been 'bureaucratically deformed'. The position was therefore more complex than Trotsky (or Bukharin) had described it. The workers were, of course, bound in duty to defend that State, and this must determine the attitude of the trade unions towards it. The unions should not indulge in systematic opposition; they must adopt a constructive attitude towards the State. But the workers were still bound to defend themselves from the State, because: (a) its policy might at times be the resultant of conflicting pressures from peasants and workers, and (b) elements of arbitrary bureaucratic rule might necessitate such acts of defence on the part of the workers. The trade unions should therefore have a measure of autonomy *vis-à-vis* the Government. Nor should adherence to the trade unions be made compulsory for the workers, as Trotsky had suggested. 'First of all,' Lenin again pleaded, 'we ought to try and prevail by persuasion and only then by coercion.'[1] Lenin as much as Trotsky, however, insisted on the 'revolutionary historical birthright of the party' and on the need for the trade unions to accept the party's guidance. The difference was one of emphasis: Trotsky dwelt more on the party's supremacy, whereas Lenin placed the greater

[1] ibid. p. 208.

stress on the democratic, voluntary, 'educational' character of the trade unions.

The difference was one of precept, not of practice. Immediately the party leadership as a whole was determined to overrule the trade unions. This was soon illustrated by a striking incident, when the Central Committee of the party demoted the most prominent Bolshevik trade unionist, Tomsky, from the trade union leadership. Such demotions were later to occur with some frequency; and the procedure adopted was as follows: the decision of the Central Committee of the party about the dismissal of, say, Tomsky, was conveyed not strictly to the All-Russian Council of Trade Unions (of which Tomsky had been the chairman) but to the Communist *fraktsya* or cell within that council. The members of the *fraktsya* were bound by the statutes of the party to act on instructions from the Central Committee. The *fraktsya* then placed a proposal for a change in the leadership before the plenary session of the Trade Union Council. The non-party members of the council might insist on retaining Tomsky as leader of the trade unions, but they could hardly carry the day. The entire *fraktsya*, including Tomsky, would vote for the proposal embodying the party's instruction. In this way the party could almost always impose its will.[1]

For all that, Lenin's insistence on relative autonomy for the trade unions was not without significance. In the combination of coercion and persuasion which Lenin envisaged, he aimed at progressively reducing the share of the former and increasing that of the latter. He hoped that economic recovery would enable the ruling party to reinfuse proletarian democracy into the proletarian dictatorship and to restore a wide measure of free expression of working-class opinion. Whether

[1] One of the charges made against Lenin and Trotsky by Shlyapnikov was that they systematically abused the *fraktsyas* inside the trade unions to overrule the opinion of Bolshevik trade unionists (ibid. p. 212).

this was practicable or not is, of course, a different question—
there were enough symptoms already to show that *ce n'est que
le provisoire qui dure*. But in his motion on the trade unions
Lenin was anxious to underline the provisional character of
the curtailment of workers' rights.

His motion was accepted by an overwhelming majority at
the Congress. For it there voted 336 delegates as against 50
who voted for Trotsky's motion and only 18 for the Workers'
Opposition. The actual division of opinion was deeper and
wider than the vote suggested. The Leninist attitude, because
of its moderate and inconclusive character, was acceptable to
various groups in the party: to the economic administrators
who wished for greater submission on the part of the trade
unions, and to trade unionists anxious to obtain more elbow
room. Whatever the motives, the view that the trade unions
should not be swallowed up by the State but that they should
voluntarily co-operate with it obtained the sanction of the
Congress. Since this conception was associated with Lenin's
name and since Lenin himself never revised it (a year later
illness removed him from the stage), it became part of the
Leninist orthodoxy, which came to be established after his
death, that the trade unions should remain a non-govern-
mental, a non-State organization. This could have some
reality, in the long run, only if the State had become more
democratic, if the idea at least of proletarian democracy had
made genuine progress. This was not to happen. As we shall
see later, in practice Trotsky's formula came to govern the
position of the trade unions in later years, in the period of
planned economy. To all intents and purposes the unions then
became part of the governmental machinery. In theory,
however, Lenin's formula, unrevised, was to remain in force.

3

The New Economic Policy

TRANSITION TO NEP

THE controversy at the tenth Congress was based on the assumption of a totally State-owned and State-managed industry. The problem whether the trade unions should or should not form part of the State was so acute precisely in this context. Yet at the same Congress Lenin initiated the New Economic Policy (NEP) which introduced a mixed, socialist-capitalist economy. Soon afterwards, private capital, Russian and foreign, was readmitted into industry and commerce, while the State retained its 'commanding posts' in large-scale industry. This change was bound to create a new situation for the trade unions. Yet by the time of the tenth Congress the implications of NEP had apparently not yet been worked out by the Bolshevik leaders.

The first consequences of NEP for the unions became apparent when their fourth Congress was convened in May 1921. Curiously enough, only the faintest echo of the recent stormy debates was heard at this national gathering of trade unionists. The Bolsheviks, having decided the issue at the Congress of the party, did not reopen it before the trade union forum. For them the matter had been settled; all members of the party, whatever their private views, had now to vote unanimously for the official resolutions. This circumstance again indicated to what extent matters of vital importance to the trade unions were now settled outside the unions. The non-Bolshevik groups at the fourth Trade Union Congress tried to provoke discussion, but with little effect. The Left Social Revolutionaries, who as a party had been banned but were

59

still allowed to act as a group at the Trade Union Congress, demanded, like the Workers' Opposition in the Bolshevik ranks, complete trade union control over industry. The Mensheviks, on the other hand, denounced the extent to which the statification of the trade unions had, regardless of Bolshevik resolutions to the contrary, already taken place; and they pressed for complete separation between trade unions and State, on the ground that under the NEP the workers would be compelled to defend themselves against private and State capitalism. The Menshevik motion also demanded free elections, freedom of speech, and freedom of action for all socialist parties in and outside the trade unions.[1] All these motions were, of course, voted down by the Bolshevik majority.

Meanwhile the scale of the revival of capitalism in industry was unknown. The Congress was confused by contradictory news and rumours about the prevailing economic chaos and the proposed readmission of private capital into industry. The spokesmen of the ruling party made conflicting forecasts. Lozovsky, who had in the meantime rejoined the Bolsheviks, spoke about the reinfiltration of foreign capitalism as compelling the trade unions to resume a militant attitude towards employers. The spokesman of the Supreme Council of National Economy, Miliutin, denied rumours about wholesale readmission of private capital into industry, but stated that factories which the Government was unable to put into operation would have to be handed over to private entrepreneurs. 'We cannot behave,' said Miliutin, 'like the dog that lies on the hay, himself does not eat it and does not let others eat it'.[2] A motion submitted by the Central Council of the Trade Unions anticipated not only the defence of workers against small capitalists but also the formation of special organs through which the trade unions would exercise

[1] 4. Syezd Profsoyuzov, p. 69 ff.   [2] ibid. p. 77.

control over privately-owned industry, a reminiscence of the 'workers' control' of 1917.[1] The prevailing attitude seems to have been that the trade unions would adopt a dual attitude, a productionist one in State-owned industry and a consumptionist one towards private employers. But it was already pointed out by delegates that such a dual attitude might be untenable: if the trade unions succeeded in raising wages and improving conditions in private industry, workers would rush from governmental to privately-owned factories.

The implications of NEP became much clearer the following year, at the eleventh Congress of the party, in March 1922, and at the fifth Congress of the Trade Unions in September. The eleventh Congress of the party reasserted the main principles of the Leninist resolution passed by the tenth Congress. But it also introduced a few essential correctives, which further curtailed the influence of the trade unions. True enough, it was now re-emphasized that the unions ought to support the claims of labour in private and leased enterprises and also in such socialized concerns where workers suffered from bureaucratic encroachments.[2] The Congress did not ban strikes, but appealed to the trade unions to refrain from calling them: 'Neither the Communist Party, nor the Soviet Government, nor the Trade Unions can forget and conceal from the workers . . . that strike action in a state with a proletarian government can be explained and justified exclusively by bureaucratic deformations of that state and by remnants of capitalism. . .'[3] If mistakes of the economic administration, backwardness of certain groups of workers, provocation by counter-revolutionary elements, or imprudence on the part of the trade unions led to labour conflicts in State-owned enterprises, the unions were obliged to do their utmost to liquidate such conflicts. In private industry they were apparently to allow labour conflicts to run their

[1] ibid. p. 66 ff.   [2] *V.K.P. (b) o Profsoyuzakh*, p. 165.   [3] ibid.

61

spontaneous course. But contrary to what the previous Congress had said on the matter, the party now resolved that 'the Trade Unions should not assume directly any functions of control over production in private businesses and in businesses leased to private hands'.[1] This was in striking contrast to the Bolshevik attitude of 1917–18, when the trade unions were entrusted with controlling privately-owned industry. The contrast was explained on the ground that in 1917–18 the machinery of the proletarian State had not yet been set up—the working class therefore had to establish control over industry mainly through the trade unions. At present the working class was in possession of its own State and controlled the entire economy through it, and not through the unions.

More important still was the decision of the eleventh Congress to eliminate the trade unions from participation in actual industrial management. Individual management instead of management by committee was now to be firmly established. 'The main . . . task of the proletariat after it has conquered power . . . is to increase the volume of output and to raise . . . the productive forces of society. . . [This] demands that the managements of the factories should concentrate full power in their hands. . . Any direct interference of the trade unions with the management of enterprises must in such circumstances be regarded as absolutely harmful and inadmissible.'[2]

The Congress dealt another blow at the trade unions when it decided that industrial managers alone should be responsible for fixing wages and rations and for the distribution of working clothes to workers, though they should do this in accordance with collective agreements concluded with trade unions. The Leninist resolution adopted by the previous Congress had made all these the joint responsibility

[1] ibid. p. 168.   [2] ibid. pp. 167–8.

of trade unions, food offices, and industrial managements.[1]

These reforms deepened a split in the Central Council of Trade Unions. Tomsky, opposed to the reforms, was temporarily removed from work at the council and ostensibly sent on a 'mission' to Turkestan. Andreev, who had backed Trotsky in the trade union debate and consistently represented the productionist viewpoint, took Tomsky's place. When Tomsky and his adherents protested that the trade unions had been reduced to impotence, the productionists replied that this was not so, because the trade unions were expected to supply an ever-growing contingent of industrial managers from their members.[2] This was true enough. But those who shared Tomsky's viewpoint argued that, although many individual trade unionists had become industrial managers, the trade unions as bodies were losing influence, especially as the workers promoted to managers tended to lose touch with their original unions. The party then urged the new worker-managers to remain good trade unionists. This was no more than a *pium desideratum*. The worker promoted to manager gradually became accustomed to approach his problems from the managerial and not the trade unionist angle. The trade unions were once again offered the consolation that they would participate in over-all economic plan-

[1] Hitherto the trade unions had been in charge of the distribution of some consumers' goods. Since wages were often still paid in kind and not in money, it was a matter of some importance who fixed rations for various categories of workers. At the fourth Congress of the Trade Unions it was stated that seven categories of rations were in existence and that the differences between them were very considerable.

[2] '(1) The Trade Unions take part in the formation of all economic and state authorities . . . putting forward their own candidates . . . [but] the power of decision belongs exclusively to the economic authorities. . . These take into account the opinions on all candidates expressed by the corresponding Trade Unions.' '(2) One of the most important tasks of any Trade Union is the promotion and training of administrators from among workers . . . if at present we have only tens of really competent industrial administrators [drafted from Trade Unions] and hundreds of more or less competent ones, we shall very soon need hundreds of the former category and thousands of the latter' (*V.K.P.* (*b*) *o Profsoyuzakh*, p. 168).

ning and advise the Government which factories should and which should not be handed over to private capital. The pill was hardly sweetened.

The new economic course was justified on grounds of expediency. But there was more to it than that. The party was now engaged in building up, on the basis of its monopoly of power, the monolithic State.[1] The subordination of the trade unions was a prerequisite as well as one of the results of that process. Yet this whole development was still in one of its initial phases. Nominally, the party still insisted on the need for the trade unions to keep the balance, so subtly drawn by Lenin, between the various aspects of their activity: persuasion and coercion; defence of the material interests of the workers and pressure on the workers for higher productivity; the need to take into account the moods of the rank and file and the need to resist those moods, when from an economic viewpoint they were not sound. 'These contradictions', stated the eleventh Congress, 'are not accidental and they cannot be removed in the course even of a number of decades.'[2] 'The aforementioned contradictions will inevitably give rise to conflicts, lack of harmony, friction, etc. A higher authority . . . is necessary to settle such conflicts at once. Such an authority is the Communist Party and the international association of the Communist Parties of all countries, the Comintern.'[3] This curious phrase meant that the trade unions had the right to appeal from the Soviet Government to the Russian Communist Party and from the latter to the Communist International. They have never made use of this right. In later years, after Stalin had firmly established himself in power, the very idea of such an appeal would have seemed wild, not only because the Comintern was completely in the

---

[1] It was not pure coincidence that on the day after the conclusion of the eleventh Congress of the party, which adopted these resolutions, Stalin was appointed General Secretary of the Central Committee.

[2] *V.K.P. (b) o Profsoyuzakh*, p. 171.   [3] ibid. p. 172.

hands of the Russian party, but because the mere thought of such an appeal smacked of treason.[1] Meanwhile it was significant that the Bolshevik leaders still anticipated that within the framework of the single-party State, now taking shape, the trade unions would for a long time to come (for a 'number of decades') maintain their relative autonomy and consequently their dual attitude towards the State.

Nevertheless, the eleventh Congress made another long step towards the complete destruction of the democratic constitution of the trade unions. It resolved that the secretaries and chairmen of the central committees of the unions must be members of the party of long standing, men who had belonged to it before the revolution. Similarly, the chairmen, secretaries, and members of the leading regional trade union bodies had also to be party members of at least three years' standing.[2] The Congress at the same time adopted one more of a series of resolutions in favour of normal elections in trade unions; but it did not say what should happen if in normal elections other than party members were elected. In practice, elections were already rigged to such an extent that the dilemma could hardly arise.

The productionist viewpoint found eloquent expression in the resolutions of the twelfth Congress of the party (April 1923), the first Congress in which Lenin did not participate:

Aiming by all means at an improvement in the condition of the working class, the state authorities and the Trade Unions ought to remember that a prolonged and all-round improvement is possible only on the basis of an expanding, that is profit-bearing industry. . . To keep in operation businesses with low employment or to keep employed in any factory a number of workers which does not correspond with the actual productivity of that factory is a wasteful and irrational form of social security and is therefore detrimental to the working class interests of to-morrow. The saddling of industrial enterprises with all sorts of overhead costs . . . dis-

---

[1] This was how the appeals of the Trotskyist Opposition from the Russian party to the Comintern were in fact treated.
[2] *V.K.P. (b) o Profsoyuzakh*, p. 173.

rupts the possibility of correct calculation and imposes . . . upon the state expenses which it is not at present in a position to bear. Arbitrary . . . 'grants' by trusts represent nothing else but wastage of governmental property and should be punished by law. . .

The appointment, transfer, and replacement of the economic personnel is the responsibility of the leading economic authorities—a necessary condition for the genuine management of industry. . . The recommendations and testimonials of the trade unions should be attentively taken into account, but they can in no case lift the responsibility [for taking decisions] from the corresponding economic authorities, to whom the existing legislation leaves complete freedom of choice and appointment.

The economic administrator is always confronted with two dangers: (a) the danger that his exacting demands may antagonize the workers, their representative bodies, the local branches of the party and Soviet institutions; and (b) the danger of taking in matters of production, wages, etc., the line of least resistance and of sacrificing thereby the profitability of the business, and consequently its future. It goes without saying that the manager of a Soviet factory ought to show the greatest attentiveness to the material and spiritual needs of the workers, to their feelings and moods. But at the same time he must not lose sight of his supreme duty towards the working class, as a whole, a duty which consists in raising productivity of labour, lowering costs of production and increasing the volume of material goods available to the proletarian state. Trade Unionists and party members ought to co-operate in every way with the Soviet manager for this purpose. Attentiveness, determination and discrimination are the indispensable qualities of the Soviet manager. But his best testimonial is the favourable balance sheet of the business.[1]

TRADE UNIONS UNDER NEP

The further evolution of the trade unions was bound up with two factors: (a) the general economic situation and the changing social structure of Russia; and (b) the political evolution of the regime, i.e. the progressive crystallization of the single-party system.

The mixed economy of NEP existed from 1921 till roughly the end of 1928, when the first Five-Year Plan was initiated. The effect upon the trade unions of the partial readmission of capitalism was not as far-reaching as had been expected.

[1] ibid. pp. 186–7. The author of this resolution was Trotsky.

In industry, capitalist enterprise regained relatively little ground. Foreign concessionaires were less interested in investment in Russia than Lenin and his colleagues had hoped. Private enterprise was strong only in trade and, of course, in farming. At the height of NEP only 18·8 per cent (1·6 out of 9·6 million) of the total number of wage and salary earners were employed in the private sector of the economy. However, although the State employed four-fifths of the mass of wage earners, the circumstance that a fraction of the working class was again employed by private capital could not but affect in some degree the outlook of the trade unions as a whole. In relation to private employers the trade unions preserved their independence and made demands on behalf of the workers. This alone tended to give them some independence in relation to the State as well, altogether apart from the fact that, in virtue of the resolutions of the last three party Congresses, the State was committed to respect their relative autonomy. The trade unions could not adopt a totally productionist attitude in governmental factories and a totally consumptionist one in private industry. Throughout the years of NEP their policy was the resultant of the two attitudes.

One of the dominant economic features of this period was mass unemployment. Due to a combination of industrial underemployment and agricultural over-population, it persisted throughout the NEP. At the height of NEP about two million people were without jobs, a very large number for a country in which total industrial employment was only 1·2 million in 1920 and 2·1 million in 1925.[1] The problem with

[1] Latent agricultural over-population was reflected in the steady growth of seasonal employment of peasants outside farming:

PEASANTS SEASONALLY EMPLOYED IN INDUSTRY

| 1923–4 | 1·7 million | 1927–8 | 4·0 million |
| 1926–7 | 3·2 million | 1928–9 | 4·3 million |

(*Bolshaya Sovetskaya Entsiklopediya*, S.S.S.R. (1948), p. 1124.)

which Russia had to contend in the next decade—that of securing, under conditions of full employment, a steady supply of fresh labour to an expanding industry—did not yet exist.

Direction of labour which had been part and parcel of military communism was no longer needed—it was in fact abandoned in February 1922. The 'reserve army of unemployed', to use the Marxian term, performed in the Russian economy of the twenties the same function which it performs in any capitalist economy: it pressed upon the wages and living conditions of the employed workers. Throughout most of this period real wages were considerably below the pre-1914 level, which was understandable in view of the disastrous impoverishment of the country. Fear of unemployment prevented workers from demanding higher wages and from pressing the trade unions to stake out claims on their behalf, claims that might have brought the unions into conflict with the employer State. In 1924 only 24,000 workers went on strike in State-owned industry; in 1925—34,000, in 1926—33,000; in 1927—20,000; and in 1928 even fewer than 20,000. This is not to say that labour conflicts in milder form were not widespread. By the end of NEP, at the eighth Congress of the Trade Unions (December 1928) Schmidt, the Commissar for Labour, stated that in the previous few years industrial conflicts had involved nearly 2·5 million workers annually. But as the workers were weary of resorting to strikes, most conflicts were settled by arbitration.

The attitude of the trade unions towards private industry fluctuated and was ambiguous. At the beginning of NEP and up to the middle twenties, private employers were often able to offer better conditions of labour than those prevailing in State-owned industry. Private capital re-entrenched itself in consumers' industries, the produce of which was in very heavy demand. The profits of private industry were sufficiently high to make it worth while for employers to raise wages.[1] The trade unions witnessed the paradox that small capitalist businesses compelled the proletarian State to compete with them in the improvement of labour conditions.[2] But this could not, of course, last very long. In the middle twenties State-owned industry was rehabilitated and reached the pre-war level of output; and so private industry was quickly losing the advantages it had enjoyed. The normal antagonism between employer and trade union returned. However, the Government, determined to speed up economic recovery, did not want to see the working of private industry interrupted by strikes. The private employers certainly worked for their profit, but the output of their factories, it was pointed out, was essential to the economic balance of the proletarian State. The trade unions, therefore, often adopted the 'productionist' attitude even in private industry.[3] But equally often, compelled to tread warily in State-owned industry, they compensated themselves by excessive militancy towards private employers, until they (i.e. trade unions) were curbed by the Government. Between these two extremes the trade unions wavered.

The NEP period saw the introduction of a mass of progressive labour legislation. But the trade unions did not regain real freedom of action, in spite of the relative liberalism in the Government's economic policy. This became striking after the recovery of industry was more or less complete. In March 1927 the Central Committee of the party ordered a

[1] This caused the fifth Congress of the Trade Unions to complain that heavy industry was at a disadvantage in its competition with light industry and to ask the Government to protect heavy industry against unfair competition.

[2] In 1922 wages in State-owned industry were increased by 100 per cent, but the increase was soon swallowed up by monetary inflation.

[3] At the seventh Congress of the Trade Unions (December 1926) Dogadov, one of the prominent leaders of that period, complained about a 'deviation' in the trade unions which consisted in the treatment of private businesses on an equal footing with the socialist ones (7. *Syezd Profsoyuzov*, p. 84).

large-scale release of redundant labour from State-owned industry.[1] The release was explained on the ground that industry was already fully utilizing its old plant and that expansion was now possible only through technical rationalization, higher efficiency, and construction of new plant. The trade unions were asked not only to agree to the release of redundant labour, but also to work out higher norms of output and to co-operate with the economic administration in the processes of rationalization. The Commissariat of Labour was to shift the released workers to new places of employment. This, of course, implied a degree of direction of labour. But for some time yet this implication was to be devoid of practical significance, because industry was still developing too slowly to require and absorb the redundant labour. The resolution of the Central Committee brought forth a vehement protest from the opposition led by Trotsky, Zinoviev, and Kamenev. One of the charges levelled against the economic administration and the trade unions was that in the scheme for rationalization the emphasis was not on higher technical efficiency but on exacting more physical exertion from the workers.[2] The trade unions, nevertheless, responded to the appeal of the Central Committee, although they did so half-heartedly and not without provoking protests from the ranks.

In their attempt to balance between the State and the workers, between the economic administration and their own rank and file, the trade unions most often inclined towards the State and the economic administration.[3] Nevertheless,

[1] *V.K.P. (b) o Profsoyuzakh*, p. 310.
[2] L. Trotsky, *The Real Situation in Russia* (London, Allen & Unwin, 1928) p. 44.
[3] Some parallel might perhaps be drawn between the position of the Soviet trade unions in those years and the attitude of the T.U.C. towards Mr Attlee's Government in 1945-9, but it would be wrong to overlook the differences in the economic and social background, since even under the NEP 80 per cent of the Soviet workers were employed in the socialist sector of the economy.

THE NEW ECONOMIC POLICY

they were in almost constant conflict with everybody: the
State, the economic administration, the party, and their own
rank and file. At the fifth Congress of the Trade Unions
Tomsky related with melancholy irony how '. . . at every
congress, conference, meeting, wherever four people assembled, the first and the most important point on the agenda is
the problem of our mutual relations. . . If you ask any
branch, sub-branch or responsible official for a report or an
organizational plan, you may rest assured that three-quarters,
or at best a good half of that report will be devoted to the
problem of our mutual relations.'[1] The fourteenth Congress
of the party (December 1925) thus rebuked the trade unions:
'It is necessary to fight against that deviation which takes the
form of a strange bloc of some Trade Unionists and Trade
Unions with the economic authorities, a bloc based on uncritical wholesale approval and defence . . . before the workers
of all measures and proposals emanating from the economic
administration. This transforms the Trade Unions into an
appendage and political department of the economic administration and leads them to forget what is their main
function.'[2] At the same time the Congress rebuked the unions
for meddling with the business of the economic administration; it also remonstrated with the economic administration
for dealing with the workers behind the back of the trade
unions. At a Congress of the Trade Unions Dogadov charged
the Supreme Council of National Economy with trying to
decree industrial wages without any reference to the unions.
At the same Congress other delegates stated that collective
bargaining had become a mere sham.[3]

The extent to which the trade unions' influence was
diminishing can be seen in their changing attitudes towards
governmental arbitration in labour conflicts. In the opening

[1] 5. *Syezd Profsoyuzov*, p. 118. [2] *V.K.P. (b) o Profsoyuzakh*, p. 271.
[3] 7. *Syezd Profsoyuzov*, p. 86 and passim.

71

years of NEP it was thought almost impossible that compulsory arbitration should be imposed upon the unions. At the fifth Trade Union Congress (1922) Schmidt, the Commissar for Labour, reported on a governmental decision investing power of arbitration in his Commissariat. The Commissar himself, as we know, was appointed on the proposal of the Central Council of Trade Unions and could in principle be dismissed by that council. Even so, the idea that he should act as an arbiter, independently of the unions, still shocked many trade unionists. And so Schmidt told the Congress that the decree on compulsory arbitration had been passed by the Government against his opinion and that he would in practice interpret it in favour of the unions.[1] Compulsory arbitration, he stated, would be applied in individual conflicts only, where no collective agreement was involved, and in cases of flagrant violation of labour legislation. If there must be arbitration, then it should be carried out not by a branch of the administration but by a special chamber, and in no case should the trade unions be denied the right to call strikes.[2] On behalf of the trade unions, Tomsky then spoke in favour of local arbitration commissions, composed of trade unionists and representatives of factory managements, and of the advisability of their referring conflicts to the local branches of the Commissariat of Labour. The trade unions, he added. would call strikes only in extreme cases.[3] Another leading trade unionist, Rudzutak, the future vice-Premier, declared that the unions would suppress unauthorized strikes, but they would insist that in all strikes backed by themselves the demands of the workers must be met, and that the administrative organs that provoked strikes must be

[1] In later years no member of the Soviet Government would have dared to reveal his disagreement with the Government. Schmidt remained Commissar for Labour for six years longer.
[2] 5. *Syezd Profsoyuzov*, p. 87.   [3] ibid. p. 105 and passim.

held responsible for this and the guilty officials must be dismissed, as a matter of principle. Some speakers at the Congress demanded that full powers of arbitration should be vested exclusively in the trade unions, but this was resisted by the Government. The debate on the whole revealed how great relatively was still the strength of the trade unions.

Three years later, in December 1925, the fourteenth Congress of the party adopted another resolution on compulsory arbitration which showed to what an extent the position of the trade unions had in the meantime changed.[1] The resolution asserted that it had become customary for the party committees, instead of the branches of the Commissariat of Labour, to arbitrate in labour conflicts. The Congress urged that this practice be discontinued. Yet the habit of those concerned to refer their conflicts to the party committees, and not to the trade unions or the Commissariat of Labour, reflected the real relationship between the respective institutions. The Congress further gave the economic administration the right to ask for compulsory arbitration and it strengthened the influence of the industrial managements in local arbitration committees. This was a far cry from Schmidt's assurance that compulsory arbitration would not be used against trade unions. The Trotsky-Zinoviev opposition commented on this reform that it '. . . reduced to nothing the collective contract itself, changing it from a two-sided act of agreement into an administrative organ. . . The past years have been characterized by a sharp increase in labour conflicts, most of them being settled by compulsory rather than by conciliatory measures.'[2] The opposition pressed for the annulment of the rights just given to the industrial managements. The trade union leaders, including Tomsky, still endorsed the extension

[1] *V.K.P. (b) o Profsoyuzakh*, p. 272 ff.
[2] Trotsky, *The Real Situation in Russia*, p. 49.

of the prerogatives of the industrial managers, but two or three years later Tomsky and his adherents were to repeat almost literally Trotsky's and Zinoviev's criticisms and demands.

4
Planned Economy

IN the years 1925–7 the Soviets reaped the fruits of NEP;
but the Bolshevik Party was divided by a bitter controversy, in which the trade unions were anything but
disinterested spectators. Trotsky, Zinoviev, and Kamenev
demanded that private enterprise should be curbed with a
stronger hand than hitherto, and that the Government should
embark upon more rapid industrialization and upon gradual
collectivization of farming. The opposition at the same time
criticized the 'bureaucratic centralism' of the regime and
demanded a return to 'proletarian democracy', in which the
trade unions would once again be free to defend the workers
against the managements.

In those years the ruling group in party and Government
still consisted of a coalition of the so-called right wing of the
party, which was in principle opposed to the demands of the
opposition, and of the centre, led by Stalin, which wavered
between the opposed wings but for the time being stuck to the
coalition with the right. The ruling circle favoured a continuation of NEP and was reluctant to embark upon rapid
industrialization and collectivization. It is difficult to say
exactly what was the attitude of the mass of trade unionists,
since they never had the chance to speak their minds frankly.
The whole dispute was conducted under immense administrative pressure against the opposition. The leadership of the
trade unions, however, sided unequivocally with the right
wing of the party and resisted demands for rapid industrialization. Tomsky, still the most authoritative leader of the
unions, was one of the three chiefs—the other two were

75

Bukharin and Rykov—of the right-wing Bolsheviks. At the Congresses of the Trade Unions which took place in this period the Trotskyist opposition (or the 'joint opposition' as it was officially called) still had its spokesmen, but the overwhelming majority of delegates, who may or may not have faithfully reflected the mood of the rank and file, voted for the official party line, as represented by Tomsky.

TRANSITION TO PLANNED ECONOMY

This lack of enthusiasm for industrialization displayed by the trade union leadership may appear puzzling. The trade unions, so it might seem, should have grasped how much they stood to gain from a policy which promised to increase the numbers of industrial workers and, generally speaking, to add weight to the industrial and trade unionist elements. Trotsky, Zinoviev, and Kamenev therefore charged the trade union leadership with lack of imagination and 'bureaucratic conservatism', charges that are so often levelled by the political sections of the labour movements against the chiefs of the trade unions in other countries as well. And indeed, the economic policy advocated by the opposition, and later applied with extreme brutality by Stalin himself, did involve enormous uncertainties and risks, which a cautious, more or less honest but narrow-minded and already routine-ridden trade union officialdom wished to avoid. But, altogether apart from this, Tomsky and his adherents had their specific reasons for viewing with anxiety the prospects of rapid industrialization.

It was, or it must have been clear to them that this would be accompanied by a further considerable increase in the powers of the economic administration as against the trade unions. For all the readiness of the unions, and of Tomsky personally, to co-operate with and to submit to the Government and the Supreme Council of National Economy, there was, as we saw, almost permanent friction between them, friction which was not necessarily harmful—it had in theory been accepted as part of the normal processes of proletarian democracy—and which was inevitable as long as the trade unions enjoyed a modicum of autonomy. The trade union leadership clung to that modicum of autonomy.

Planned industrialization implied direction of labour. When the issue was posed in the middle twenties, it was a theoretical point only, in view of the large unemployment still existing. But it was not difficult to foresee that with expansion of industry unemployment would vanish, and that the next problem would be how to secure additional labour. The trade union leaders must also have been aware that rapid industrialization demanded the expansion of producers' industries, in the first instance. The individual worker was immediately interested in the development of consumers' industries, and the union leaders tended to voice his consumptionist bias. Apart from such strictly trade unionist considerations, Tomsky and the right-wing Bolsheviks were apprehensive of the ruthlessness with which the new policy, if adopted, was likely to be sponsored.

Tomsky gave all these reasons for his opposition in a speech at the eighth Congress of the Trade Unions (December 1928). Stalin had just fallen out with the right wing of the party and sponsored the first Five-Year Plan; and this was the last time that Tomsky appeared at a Congress as the recognized leader of the trade unions. He revealed that industry had been troubled by many unofficial strikes which had been due to the 'Trade Unions paying inadequate attention to the needs of the masses, to their being detached from the masses and showing contempt for the small matters of the workers' life'.[1] He demanded real elections in the unions, implying that hitherto elections had been rigged. The rank and file, he went on, were afraid of speaking their minds, because critics were sure to be labelled Mensheviks or counter-

[1] *8. Syezd Profsoyuzov*, p. 24 and passim.

77

revolutionaries.[1] The friction between the trade unions and
the economic administration had been getting worse. The
economic administration had been pressing down the level
of wages and failing to observe collective agreements. It was
the industrial managements rather than the unions that
needed more discipline. 'There should be no friendship,'
Tomsky said, 'between the economic administrator and the
Trade Unionist, when it comes to carrying out the collective
agreement—both sides must fulfil their commitments.' 'Very
often pathetic things are concealed behind planning. Planning is often understood in this way: "Talk according to plan,
do not say a word which is not according to plan".' Factory
meetings were convened only three times a year; even
so they were regarded as a nuisance by industrial managers.
The resolutions of the party which had urged systematic
education of workers in the administration of the national
economy had not been honoured. Planned economy,
Tomsky argued just as Trotsky had done some time earlier,
could not properly function without some freedom of discussion, for only through discussion was it possible to correct
mistakes and bring precision into the plans. He did not
discard the productionist attitude in principle, and he re-
peated emphatically that the trade unions need not be
ashamed of pressing workers for higher productivity, but this
pressure 'must take civilized forms. . . This means that you
and we have left behind the period of military communism,
when . . . in some Trade Unions they set up gaols [i.e. for
their undisciplined members]. This, of course, was no
civilized form of action, when Trade Unions together with
managers imposed disciplinary punishment upon the workers.'[2] Tomsky was supported in the debate by other spokesmen, among them by the representative of the most important

[1] ibid. p. 38.
[2] ibid. pp. 42, 44, and passim. It is surprising to see that the Webbs
attributed to Tomsky the view that 'It was not for the Trade Unions to
press for improvements in factory technique, even if these would lead to

78

trade union, that of the metal workers, who spoke about the disregard shown for the needs of the consumers.[1]

The case for rapid industrialization was made by Kuibyshev, Orjonikidze, Zhdanov, and other leaders of the Stalinist group. Kuibyshev acquainted the Congress with one of the early variants of the first Five-Year Plan and made a striking comparison between the productivity of the American and the Russian workers. He said that whereas the output of one American worker at the furnace was 3,300 tons of steel per year, the output of the Russian worker was only 330 tons, exactly one-tenth. This comparison provided an index of Russian industrial backwardness.[2] The country could not overcome that backwardness as long as it was satisfied with industrialization 'at the snail's pace', advocated by right-wing Bolsheviks. According to another spokesman, the Five-Year Plan provided for a 95 per cent increase in productivity of labour, which in the case given by Kuibyshev would still have left Russian productivity at one-fifth of the American. The economic administration could not but press for higher output; and—this was the unspoken but obvious conclusion —it could not be very choosy about the forms of that pressure.[3]

Dramatic as was the controversy on the floor of the Congress, the real fight took place not there but at a closed

increased productivity', and to describe him as an advocate of an 'anarchic scramble after rises in wages . . . irrespective of their effect on the required universal increase of industrial productivity . . .' (Sidney and Beatrice Webb, *Soviet Communism* [London, Longmans, 1944], p. 131). This is, of course, an uncritical repetition of the official distortions and charges directed against Tomsky. Another echo of an official legend is the Webbs' assertion that the purpose of the anti-Tomsky purge in the trade unions was to remove unco-operative persons 'not sprung from the manual labour class' (loc. cit.). Whether any of the disputants was of working-class origin was completely irrelevant to this controversy, but what the Webbs apparently did not know is that for many years Tomsky had been the only authentic worker among the members of the Politbureau.

[1] *8. Syezd Profsoyuzov*, p. 96.   [2] ibid. p. 373 and passim.
[3] Kuibyshev denied the statement made by Tomsky's adherents that the Government had started the new policy of industrialization with a cut in the social services.

session of the Communist *fraktsya*, that is, at a conference of the Communist delegates to the Congress. The *fraktsya* followed the Politbureau's instruction not to re-elect Tomsky as chairman of the Central Council. The Stalinist group in the trade union leadership was strengthened by the election of Kaganovich to the council—Kaganovich was the main driving power behind the subsequent purge in the unions. The nominal successor to Tomsky as chairman of the council was Shvernik, who was later to become present President of the U.S.S.R. Schmidt, the Commissar for Labour, who was inclined towards the right-wing Bolsheviks, announced at the Congress his resignation from the commissariat.[1]

The eighth Congress of the Trade Unions, and even more so the sixteenth conference of the party which took place four months later, in April 1929, opened a new chapter in the history of the trade unions and indeed of the Soviet regime at large.[2] A long series of controversies had been brought to an end. After the Trotskyist opposition, the group of Bukharin, Rykov, and Tomsky was silenced. Henceforth no open discussion of policy would be permitted. The totalitarian

[1] It was during this debate that A. Zhdanov, then known only as one of the leaders of Communist Youth, moved into the limelight. He was 'in the front line' of the attack against the right-wing Bolsheviks. It was he who from the floor of the Congress demanded Tomsky's dismissal. Yaglom, the editor of *Trud*, the official organ of the trade unions, in the course of a turbulent exchange spoke about Zhdanov's 'Hottentot morals', while Tomsky spoke of Zhdanov as a 'good but superficial man' wasting his considerable talents in the wrong causes (*8. Syezd Profsoyuzov*, p. 177).

[2] A resolution of the sixteenth conference stated *inter alia*: '. . . in Trade Union problems Bukharin, Rykov and Tomsky are prepared to oppose in the most dangerous fashion the Trade Unions to the party, actually aiming at the weakening of party leadership in the Unions, blurring defects in the work of the Unions, defending craft trends and the manifestations of bureaucratic ossification in parts of the Trade Union machinery, and presenting the party's struggle against these defects as a Trotskyist 'shake up' of the Trade Unions . . .' Referring to Tomsky's demand for freedom of expression, the resolution stated: 'The party . . . rejects with determination such "freedom" of criticism which the right elements demand in order to defend their anti-Leninist political line' (*V.K.P. (b) v Profsoyuzakh*, p. 389).

State with its rigid uniformity and absolute discipline, under a single leader, had taken final shape. True enough, the clauses of the old Leninist resolutions of 1921 and 1922, which guaranteed the trade unions their relative freedom, were never declared null and void, for the regime, professing a strict Leninist orthodoxy, could not openly discard a principle established by Lenin himself. But the relative autonomy of the trade unions could have no meaning when no institution and no organization whatsoever could maintain even a shred of independence *vis-à-vis* the State. To be sure, the single-party system had been in existence at least since the end of the civil war—all opposition parties had been suppressed by then. Yet in the early twenties the Bolshevik leaders were still inclined to regard that suppression as an emergency measure to be reversed as soon as the regime regained enough stability to tolerate organized opposition. And in those years Mensheviks, Social Revolutionaries, and other anti-Bolshevik groups still enjoyed some freedom of expression and organization inside the trade unions, even though their parties had been banned.[1] In the middle twenties the open controversies inside the ruling party continued to prevent the regime from acquiring the monolithic outlook. Thus, although the basis for the totalitarian State had been laid during and after the civil war, it took nearly a decade before the whole edifice grew up. In the course of that decade the trade unions availed themselves of such margins of freedom and relative independence as there were. Now, towards the end of the twenties, those margins vanished.

TRADE UNIONS AND PLANNED ECONOMY

Towards the end of 1928 the first Five-Year Plan was proclaimed. Unlike previous plans, emanating from the *Gosplan*,

---

[1] Thus, for instance, the compositors' and printers' union in Moscow was led by the Mensheviks as late as 1923.

the central planning authority, which were no more than loose prognostications, this Plan had the character of a 'law', enforced by the Government upon the whole country. Planning included labour policy, and consequently the activity of the trade unions was now strictly confined within the limits set to it.

The problem with which the planners had to contend over the greater part of the period under discussion was the extreme shortage of industrial labour, especially of skilled. In the effort to overcome this, the Government gradually worked out a very wide assortment of methods, in the application of which the trade unions played a crucial part.

As stated before, direction of labour was abolished in 1922; and up to the Second World War it was never *nominally* re-enacted. In actual fact, however, more and more elements of compulsory direction were introduced in the course of the three pre-war Five-Year Plans. Moreover, some of the forms of direction of labour were much more drastic than any of those that had been associated with militarization of labour during the civil war. The notorious mammoth forced labour camps, which came into existence during the thirties, are a case in point. From a legislative viewpoint, the fact that the Soviet Government, in spite of such drastic and brutal practices, up to the Second World War never claimed for itself overall powers of direction of labour, represents a curious anomaly. For this the Leninist orthodoxy, to which Stalinism had committed itself, was responsible: Lenin, we remember, had dismissed compulsory direction of labour and the use of the trade unions for this purpose as unjustifiable in a socialist regime, under normal conditions. This principle came to be enshrined in the party tradition, and to it the Stalinist regime had to pay its tribute. In theory, labour remained 'free'. Elements of direction were introduced on an increasing scale and ever more brutally, but in a way that should not openly clash with precept. This extreme discrepancy between precept and practice imparted to the Stalinist labour policy that strong streak of hypocrisy which was entirely lacking in the labour policy of military communism, including Trotsky's militarization of labour. Under military communism the powers of the Government and the limits to which it went to enforce them were at least known, and they were the object of discussion and criticism. This alone provided a safeguard against gross abuses, a safeguard which has not been available to the Russian workers under the evasive policies of the thirties and forties.

Given the purposes of national policy which the Soviet Government had set itself when it embarked upon rapid industrialization, a degree of direction of labour was practically inevitable. At the beginning of the first Five-Year Plan this need was in part revealed and in part veiled by the fact that, while industry was already experiencing an acute shortage of labour, the labour exchanges still registered more than a million of unemployed. In December 1929 the Central Committee of the party instructed the Central Council of the Trade Unions to find out 'within the shortest possible time what were the needs for skilled labour in various branches of industry and transport and in the various regions of the country . . . and to find out what were the changes in the composition and training of labour caused by the reconstruction and rationalization of industry'. The trade unions were also expected to help in the '. . . working out of a system of measures guaranteeing the timely and full supply of skilled labour. . .'[1] The Commissariat of Labour and the trade unions were further instructed to check the registered unemployment and to find out how much of it was real and how much was illusory. In the course of 1930 unemployment virtually disappeared, and the Government was confronted with a new problem: how to expand industry rapidly, while

[1] *V.K.P. (b) o Profsoyuzakh*, pp. 459–68.

the actual industrial labour force of the nation was already fully employed. There was, first and foremost, the question how to increase the total labour force, and then—the more specific issue: how to increase the supply of skilled labour.

(a) *Industrial Recruitment.* The solution to the first problem lay in transferring the surplus man-power of an over-populated countryside into the old and new industrial centres. This had been, broadly speaking, the main source from which other countries in the process of industrialization had drawn their man-power. But in those countries masses of migrant peasants were drawn into the *laissez-faire* mechanism of supply and demand on labour markets; and the unregulated, 'spontaneous' supply of labour dictated up to a point the rhythm of industrialization. Other circumstances being equal, scarcity of labour slowed down industrialization, whereas an over-abundant supply speeded it up, at the expense of the living standard of the working population. The Soviet Government was determined itself to dictate the tempo of industrialization, which it could not do unless it regulated the transfer of the rural surplus population into industry. This was arranged in the following way: industrial managements concluded annual agreements with the managements of collective farms, under which the latter were obliged to supply specified numbers of their 'redundant members' to the factories, mines, etc. Through this 'organized intake' of labour, industry received between 1·5 million and 2 million new workers annually, throughout the pre-war Five-Year periods. Thus was made possible a phenomenal influx of the rural population into the cities and towns of the Soviet Union, an influx for which hardly a single historic precedent can be found—it involved 24 million people between 1926 and 1939.[1]

[1] The total growth of the urban population in the same period, including the normal increase in the town-dwelling population, amounted to nearly 30 million.

The contracts between factories and collective farms were to be strictly voluntary. This they were—in part. Rural over-population was only too real, and it became even more pronounced when the collective farms were mechanized and much more new labour was 'set free'. That the great mass of raw peasants had no need to wander helplessly in search of work in remote cities, that it had no need to experience the lot of migrant peasants exposed to the horrors of early capitalist industrial revolutions, might have been of obvious social advantage. From this angle, the Soviet Government could make a very strong case for the 'organized recruitment' of peasant labour.[1] On the other hand, there was massive compulsion. The individual peasant singled out as redundant by the chairman of the collective farm had no choice but to leave; he was as good as expropriated; and he had to go to the factory or mine to which he was directed, although once there he was, as a rule, free to change his job.

A much more rigid method of 'organized intake' was enforced shortly before the German invasion of Russia, when the Government considered it necessary to increase even more rapidly than hitherto the reserves of industrial man-power. Under the decree on the State Labour Reserves, of 2 December 1940, chairmen of collective farms were obliged to call up for the labour reserves specified numbers of young men. The quotas were somewhat oddly fixed: 20 boys between 14–15 years and 2 between 16–17 for every 100 members of any collective farm aged between 14 and 55 years.[2] In proportion to the young members of the collective farms the number of those called up was, of course, very high; and the method of

[1] This does not apply, of course, to the forced labour camps, among the inmates of which political offenders or suspects formed a very high, perhaps the highest, proportion. But the forced labour camp is a monstrous excess, not the typical form of Soviet direction of labour. The typical form is precisely this 'organized intake' of peasant labour, on the basis of contracts between the industrial concerns and collective farms.

[2] *Pravda*, 3 October 1940.

recruitment resembled the manner in which Russians had been called up for the army a hundred years before under Tsar Nicholas I.

In this 'organized intake' of peasant labour the trade unions played and still play an important auxiliary role. The contracts with the collective farms are signed by the industrial managements. But the trade union, or more strictly the factory committee—its basic unit—acts as a sort of recruiting agent. Like every recruiting agent, it tries to make the industrial job look as attractive as possible in the eyes of the recruit. But, unlike the recruiting agent of the early capitalist industrial revolution, it continues to watch and, within limits, protect the recruit at the factory. The trade union is in part or entirely responsible for inuring the new-comer to labour discipline and imparting to him the habits and rudimentary skills of the industrial worker. It sees to it that the wages of the recruit, however low he may be in the scale, should at any rate not be lower than those paid to any worker of no higher skill and diligence. Nominally, the trade unions are also jointly responsible for the housing of the new workers, which in most cases was and still is abominable; and they are actually responsible for such matters as the protection of their labour, social insurance, etc. By standards of old-time trade unionism the functions of the Russian trade unions are highly mixed. No self-respecting union in the capitalist countries would act as the recruiting agent for the industrial management; but, on the other hand, few trade unions have ever concerned themselves with the raw industrial recruit (as distinct from the skilled or half-skilled and settled worker) as the Soviet trade unions have.

The organized transfer of the rural surplus population to the industrial centres solved the one great problem, without which rapid industrialization would have been impossible: it supplied industry with an almost automatically expanding

86

reserve of man-power. But it did not solve another no less vital problem—it did not secure stability of employment. Over many years Soviet industry suffered from the so-called fluidity of labour, the real scourge of the Russian economy in the thirties. Indeed, the effect of industrialization was greatly diminished by that fluidity. Workers refused to stay on their jobs; they constantly shifted from mine to mine and from factory to factory. This peculiarly Soviet phenomenon affected, as we shall see later, skilled as well as unskilled labour, but it was most characteristic for the millions of peasants drawn into industry. The causes and effects of 'fluidity' and the problems which it created for the trade unions are not difficult to gauge. In general, the poor living conditions, and quite especially the desperate shortage of housing in the cities and towns, which had been unprepared for the formidable influx of a new population, made for instability of labour. Workers moved from place to place in search of better living conditions. There was also the lack of industrial tradition and discipline in the proletarianized peasantry. All the habits of settled industrial life, regulated by the factory siren, that had in other countries been imparted to the working class over generations, often with the help of ruthless legislation—all those habits were conspicuously lacking in Russia. The peasant, who had been accustomed to work in his field according to the rhythm of nature, to toil from sunrise to sunset in the summer and to sleep through most of the winter, had now to be forced and conditioned into an entirely new routine of work. Against that he revolted and restlessly shifted from place to place. The threat of unemployment, which so often prevents a worker from leaving even the most unsatisfactory job, was absent. The fears which the *laissez-faire* mechanism of supply and demand of labour normally produced and impressed upon the mind of the worker were not there to chain the Soviet worker to the bench; and new fears were not yet substituted for the old ones. On the other hand, the Soviet worker was not free to struggle for the improvement of his living conditions as the worker in other countries had struggled under the leadership of the trade unions: he could not strike. The Soviet trade union firmly discouraged strikes, and behind the union stood the political police. Fluidity of labour was the substitute for strikes. The workers did not now coalesce to down tools. Instead, the individual worker or millions of workers individually downed tools and left their places of work to hire themselves elsewhere.

The effect of fluidity was to hamper the acquisition of industrial skill by the new worker, to disturb the functioning of industry and to make the very basis of planning uncertain. The fact that throughout the thirties fluidity was the central point of every discussion on labour policy, the subject of innumerable exhortations, instructions, and decrees, shows to what extent this spontaneous and unforeseen process obstructed the working of the planned economy. The resulting confusion was up to a point inevitable in the circumstances, but it was made even worse than it need have been by inconsistencies of policy and a neglect of consumers' needs, which only an autocratic administration could afford.

Direction of labour was at first confined to the initial stage of supplying labour to industry, i.e. to the transfer of people from the countryside to the industrial centres. At the next stage direction ceased, or at any rate ceased to be effective.

A brief survey of the measures taken by the Government and the trade unions to overcome fluidity will perhaps not be out of place here. The Government was first alarmed by this development in the latter part of 1930. On 3 September, the Central Committee of the party dealt with it in its message on the third year of the first Five-Year Plan.[1] It appealed to the trade unions (and to other organizations) to take

[1] *V.K.P.* (*b*) *o Profsoyuzakh*, p. 506.

specific measures against fluidity. It proposed that workers drafted into industry should accept the obligation to remain in their factories for specified periods, that special incentives be offered to those who honoured the obligation, and that notorious 'deserters from production' be placed under boycott by the trade unions and other bodies. At the same time it was decided to abolish the labour exchanges which had apparently facilitated 'desertion', by enabling any worker who had left his job to register for unemployment assistance and to find a new job.

A few weeks later, in October 1930, the Central Committee, realizing that exhortation was not enough, proposed specific incentives and deterrents calculated to ensure stability of labour. Workers who stayed on the same job for two years were to receive somewhat longer holidays than others; and the penalty imposed on 'deserters' and absentees was the loss of the right to industrial employment for six months.[1] The incentives were still feeble. The deterrents would have been all too powerful had it not been for the endemic character of fluidity; industrial managers, chronically short of labour and desperately anxious to reach their targets of output, were certain to disregard the sanctions decreed and to give a job to any 'deserter' from another factory who applied for one. Incidentally, the same instruction by which 'deserters' were deprived of the right of employment urged the Central Council of Trade Unions to see that no administrative pressure or compulsion should be exerted in order to make workers enter into obligations for long-term employment. This injunction once again illustrated the dilemmas of an administration which was compelled by policy and circumstance to resort to direction of labour and yet was anxious to maintain the appearance that it was not doing so.

At the beginning of the second Five-Year Plan (1933)

[1] ibid. p. 516.

fluidity of labour was as widespread and severe as ever, even though sanctions introduced in the meantime included the denial to 'deserters' of ration cards, living quarters, and so on. A resolution issued under the joint authority of Government and party, and signed by Molotov and Stalin on 8 April 1933, indicated the extent of the trouble in the coal industry of the Donetz Basin, on whose output depended the fulfilment or non-fulfilment of the Five-Year Plan. The resolution stated that:

according to the information of the statistical offices, 423,000 workers and employees left the mines in 1932. During the same period 458,000 workers and employees entered employment. In January of 1933 alone, 32,000 left and 35,000 workers and employees entered employment. This means that a considerable part of workers and employees, if not the majority, drifts restlessly from mine to mine, from the mines into the countryside, and from the countryside into the mines rather than work. . . It goes without saying that in view of such fluidity it is impossible to assimilate, if only in a half-satisfactory manner, the new technique and to master the new machines. Yet the mastery of the new technique is the key to the rise of the entire coal industry of the Donbas.[1]

[The disorder indicated] would not have taken place, if the managers of the pits . . . had given effect to the law against loiterers and absentees and deprived them of their ration cards and the right to living quarters. . .[2]

Five years later, at the beginning of the third Five-Year Plan (1938), the same disorder was still plaguing Soviet industry. New and more drastic measures were taken to tie the worker to his workshop, and these were enforced directly by the trade unions. The whole system of social insurance was remodelled so as to help to promote stability of labour; and, as the trade unions had (in 1933) been made responsible for the administration of the social insurance funds,[3] they were the chief executors of the new policy.

A decree of 28 December 1938, signed by Stalin (for the party), Molotov (for the Government), and Shvernik (for the trade unions) embodied the following provisions:[4]

[1] ibid. p. 545.   [2] ibid. pp. 546-7.   [3] See page 117, below.
[4] V.K.P. (b) o Profsoyuzakh, pp. 594-601.

90

The worker's right to a holiday with pay after five and a half months' employment was abolished—henceforth holidays were to be granted only after eleven months of uninterrupted work.

Notorious 'loiterers' and absentees were to be unconditionally dismissed from jobs.

'A worker or employee guilty of coming late to work without a valid reason, of leaving for lunch too early or returning too late, of leaving the factory or office before time or idling during working hours is liable to administrative prosecution: to be rebuked or rebuked with notice of dismissal; to be transferred to a job with less pay for three months; or to be altogether transferred to a lower grade. A worker or employee guilty of committing three such offences in one month, or four in two consecutive months, is dismissed as . . . an offender against the law of labour and labour discipline.'[1] Industrial managers failing to impose the prescribed punishments were themselves made liable to dismissal or prosecution.

The payment of insurance allowances to workers temporarily incapacitated was, under the same decree, made dependent on the length of time during which the person concerned stayed in his or her job.[2] Only after six years of permanent employment was 100 per cent of the wage or salary to be paid to the incapacitated; 80 per cent was paid after three to six years; 60 per cent after two to three years; and only 50 per cent if the worker or employee had stayed in his job less than two years.[3] (These allowances were paid to members of trade unions. Non-members received only 50

[1] ibid. p. 596.
[2] The sanctions did not, of course, apply to workers who changed jobs by order or permission of their superiors.
[3] In the coal industry allowances were more liberal. Coal-getters received 100 per cent after two years, and 60 per cent after less than two years of permanent employment.

per cent of the appropriate rates. Thus, although membership of the trade unions was, in accordance with the Leninist principle, nominally voluntary, it carried with it substantial material benefits, and non-membership entailed equally substantial loss.)

Pensions for permanent invalids were also graded in relation to the length of employment. In addition to the basic pension, bonuses were granted to invalids with satisfactory employment records. To give one example, invalids of the 'first category' (i.e. those who had been employed in mines, underground, or in harmful occupations) received 10 per cent over and above the pension after 3–5 years of permanent employment in one concern, 20 per cent after 5–10 years, and 25 per cent after more than 10 years.[1] Since all these measures were certain not only to reduce fluidity of labour, but also to reduce the sum total of pensions paid out by the trade unions, the latter were instructed to use the saved money for building additional houses for workers.

Perhaps the most drastic provision of the decree was that people who had left their jobs without permission or been guilty of grave offences against labour discipline were 'liable to compulsory administrative eviction [from their dwellings] within 10 days, without any living quarters being provided for them'.[2] Since houses, as a rule, belonged to municipalities or other public corporations, the evicted offender had practically no chance to obtain new quarters. Often this entailed deportation to a forced labour camp. The fear of the forced labour camp came now to play the role that the fear of unemployment had played under capitalism—it maintained labour discipline. This stage, however, was reached only in the latter part of the thirties, when mass deportation of political suspects, too, became a normal practice. Yet even

[1] For a more detailed scale of bonuses see *V.K.P.* (*b*) *o Profsoyuzakh*, p. 599.   [2] ibid. p. 598.

now the slender pretence that workers were not tied to their workshops was still kept up. The decree just quoted states *inter alia* that workers desiring to leave their jobs ought to give one month's notice of their intention, as if they had still been free to carry out such an intention. More curiously still, some of these legislative measures were introduced by the Government allegedly in response to demands from the trade unions themselves.

(*b*) *Training of Labour.* With the progress of industrialization and the enforcement of Draconic legislation, fluidity of labour tended to weaken, if not to disappear altogether. In the late thirties complaints about fluidity became less frequent, and after the Second World War they became rare. A considerable proportion of the 20 millions or so of the industrial proletariat already consisted of people who had acquired, if only recently, the habits and outlook of industrial workers, and were capable of imparting these to newcomers from the countryside.[1] Government, industry, and trade unions had also acquired considerable experience in handling the influx of new and raw labour. In addition, the recruits now drafted into industry were no longer quite the same raw, backward *muzhiks* of the early thirties, who had never handled a machine. The mechanized collective farm became the first training ground for industrial workers. Thus the most painful phase of the industrial revolution, and some of its ugliest repercussions in labour policy, should have been largely left behind.

For the history of the Soviet trade unions and labour policy the period of the initial accumulation of industrial skill in the rapidly growing working class presents enormous interest.

[1] The total number of workers and employees was approaching 30 million before the Second World War (it was about 33 million in 1949), but it has never been stated how many of these were manual workers and how many were office employees. Indirect indications suggest that industrial workers formed about two-thirds or slightly more of the total.

93

The problem was first tackled on a fairly large scale towards the end of 1929, when the trade unions, jointly with the Supreme Council of National Economy and the Commissariat of Education, started experimental factory schools, where cadres of skilled workers were trained without interrupting normal work at the bench. From this developed the system of *fabzavuchi*, the factory school which played an important role in later years. At the same time, the Central Committee of the party decreed that the technical colleges and schools should have at least 70 per cent of workers among their pupils.[1] The Central Council of Trade Unions organized general educational courses—it was essential for industrialization that the general standards of education be raised. The cost of those courses was borne by the trade unions, whose revenue was assured—the economic administration deducted 2 per cent of workers' wages as membership fees for the unions.[2] The trade unions were also responsible for choosing from among the workers candidates for technical schools of all grades. They distributed scholarships among their advanced members who had shown diligence and technical ability and displayed initiative at so-called factory production meetings.[3] As the rapidly expanding industry badly needed managerial personnel the Central Council of the Trade Unions was also asked to submit a list of 1,500–2,000 of its ablest organizers for promotion to managerial posts.

A year later, in 1930, economic development was so severely impeded by the shortage of skilled labour that trade unions were ordered to prepare, within twenty days, a practical plan for the training of labour in 1931. It was estimated that the additional demand for skilled labour in the

[1] *V.K.P.* (*b*) *o Profsoyuzakh*, p. 450.
[2] In the late thirties the membership fee was reduced to 1 per cent of wages.
[3] See p. 126, below.

94

basic industries alone would amount to 1·3 million men in the course of that year. These were trained in the *fabzavuchi* and technical schools in a manner which was of necessity extremely hasty and superficial. At the same time the trade unions helped the Commissariat of Labour to comb out inessential industries for skilled labour, which was to be directed to essential industries. The trade unions further established a permanent register of skilled workers which enabled them to respond instantaneously to the demands of the economic administration for labour. The pressure under which industry was working was illustrated by the fact that the Central Committee of the party now prohibited the promotion of skilled workers to administrative posts, the prohibition being valid for two years. Industrial managers were made liable to prosecution for obstructing or delaying the transfer of skilled workers, for the improper use of skilled labour, for luring workers and technicians from other undertakings by offers of higher wages, and for employing more workers than was allowed by governmentally-fixed standards. [1]

Along these and similar lines the programme for training labour developed throughout the thirties. It culminated in the 1940 decree on State Labour Reserves which ordered *inter alia* that a high proportion of those called up for industrial labour be directed to training schools. In the same year were opened 1,500 such schools, training 800,000 pupils; and for the following years the programme provided for the training of one million apprentices annually. This system worked throughout the war. It will be remembered that the State Labour Reserves consisted of boys in their middle teens. When war broke out the following year, these were too young to be called up for the forces, but vast numbers of them had already received sufficient training to fill gaps in industrial man-power caused by the mobilization of the

[1] *V.K.P.* (*b*) *o Profsoyuzakh*, p. 515.

95

older age-groups. It was to a large extent with the help of that juvenile labour that Soviet industry kept its wheels turning during the war.

(c) '*Socialist Emulation*'. In its striving for higher efficiency Soviet industry gradually came to rely upon 'socialist emulation' and upon an elaborate system of incentive wages.

At the beginning of 1929 the sixteenth party conference initiated 'socialist emulation' *en masse*. The idea dated back to the first years of the Soviet regime. The sixteenth conference in fact recalled the following words from a resolution adopted by the ninth Congress of the party (1920):

> Every social system . . . has had its own methods and ways of labour compulsion and education for labour in the interest of the exploiting classes.
>
> The Soviet order is confronted with the task . . . of developing its own methods, designed to raise the intensity and efficiency of labour on the basis of a socialized economy and in the interests of the whole people.
>
> On a par with the propaganda of ideas, which should influence the mind of the toiling masses, and with repressive measures, used against deliberate idlers, drones and disorganizers, emulation is the most powerful means towards raising productivity of labour.
>
> In capitalist society emulation had had the character of competition and had led to the exploitation of man by man. In a society in which the means of production have been nationalized, emulation in labour ought, without impinging upon the solidarity [of workers] only to raise the sum total of the products of labour.
>
> Emulation between factories, regions, shops, workshops and individual workers should be the object of careful organization and attentive research on the part of the Trade Unions and the economic administration.[1]

A serious ideological dilemma was implicit in this idea of emulation. It will be noted that the resolution just quoted stressed that the workers' emulation in production should not 'impinge upon their solidarity'. This proviso implicitly

---

[1] ibid. p. 414. The author of this resolution was Trotsky, although the same idea was frequently expounded also by Lenin. There was a touch of irony in the fact that Trotsky's words, without the authorship being mentioned, were approvingly quoted in the solemn message of the sixteenth party conference only a few weeks after the Politbureau had expelled Trotsky from Russia.

referred back to Marx's theory of the development of the modern industrial working class, given in his *Misère de la Philosophie* and in other writings. Marx distinguished two historic stages, not strictly separated from one another but rather overlapping, in the evolution of the proletariat. In the first, the outlook of the working class is characterized primarily by individualistic competition between its members. In the workshop and factory members of an immature working class compete with one another for jobs, better wages, etc. They have not yet learned to act in solidarity. They are still opposed to one another and only individually opposed to their employers. In the next phase, marked by the emergence of trade unions and other class organizations, competition between individual members of the working class tends to give place to their solidarity *vis-à-vis* the capitalists. This supersession of competition by solidarity reflects the growing maturity of the proletariat, enables it to overcome centrifugal tendencies in its own midst and to act as a class. This broad view of the evolution of the working class, which became part and parcel of the socialist and communist outlook, presupposed, of course, that in a socialist regime competition between individual members of the working class would tend to disappear, making room for full solidarity first of the workers and then of all members of a classless society.

No wonder that in the first Bolshevik appeals for socialist emulation mental reservations could be read between the lines. Emulation was 'not to impinge upon solidarity'. Emulation may take various forms: there ought to be emulation between factories, regions, shops, and workshops; that is, between collectives; but—in the last instance—it should also develop between individual workers. Its purpose was to be 'only to raise the sum total of the products of labour'. Who will produce more and better? But already behind these first appeals there loomed the tricky question whether

97

those who produce more and better should also receive higher rewards? At first the dilemma presented itself in the dimmest of forms; and the answers were tentative and at times self-contradictory. One answer, formulated by Lenin, was that if there was to be competition, that is, inequality in production (if some people were to produce more than others), then there must also be inequality in consumption. Otherwise there would be no incentive to higher production. The levellers (among whom Trotsky might be classed only with the strongest of qualifications) argued in favour of 'shock methods' in production and equality in consumption. But in those early years all Bolshevik leaders were levellers in the sense that, even when they admitted the need for differential wages in the period of transition to socialism, they still saw in the gradual equalization of wages the *sine qua non* of socialist labour policy.

This egalitarian frame of mind was still very strong when, in 1929, the sixteenth party conference, already under Stalin's exclusive leadership, launched its full-scale campaign for 'socialist emulation'. The conference still appealed, mainly if not exclusively, to the communist idealism of the working masses rather than to their *immediate* interests. It stated that 'the Trade Unions and the economic organs ought to adopt a broad system of incentives'.[1] But the incentives proposed were mainly of a moral character, designed to spur the worker's ambition and to stir his imagination. 'The names of the best workers, best specialists, best economic administrators and agronomists, the names of factories and mines and of the best Soviet and collective farms ought to become known to the entire country. . . The heroic traditions of the past years have been preserved and enriched by the working class of our country. The Leninist idea of "the organization of emulation on socialist principles" finds an ever more

[1] *V.K.P.* (*b*) *o Profsoyuzakh*, p. 415.

98

practical realization. The principles of a communist attitude towards labour begin to strike ever deeper roots', etc., etc.[1] The emphasis so far was on emulation between collective bodies rather than individual workers. Material rewards were to be given primarily to collective bodies, factories, regions, and so on. The emulation took the form of factories challenging one another to raise and improve output. These practices tended all too quickly to become stale routine or unproductive pageantry, and the trade unions were urged to take care of the economic realities behind the reports on emulation.

In 1930–1 the emphasis shifted to emulation between individual workers and to individual material rewards for records achieved in production. The shock-worker, the industrial record-man, became in a sense the central figure of Russian society. The trade unions proclaimed an All-Union Day of the Shock-Worker (or the *udarnik*) on 1 October 1930. In this movement there was undoubtedly a strong streak of idealism. The young worker was encouraged in the hope that a few years of unsparing exertion on his part would transform the whole country, modernize it, and make it into a 'Socialist America'. The trade unions displayed much initiative and shrewd propagandist techniques in promoting emulation. At the same time the shock-worker was given a privileged position. In the factories special canteens and restaurants were opened exclusively for the *udarniki*; and they were immeasurably better supplied than the canteens for ordinary workers. Better living quarters, facilities for education and rest, better supplies of rare consumer goods and so on were reserved for shock-workers and their families. Socialist emulation began most drastically to 'impinge upon solidarity'; and soon a radical revision of wages policy followed.

[1] ibid. p. 415–16.

(*d*) *Wages Policy*. Very early in the NEP period the Soviet Government enunciated the principle that the national wages bill must be closely related to the size of the national income, or rather, to its most important co-determinant—efficiency of labour. This rule was in general terms laid down by the twelfth Congress of the party (1923). In a more specific and emphatic form it was reiterated by a plenary conference of the party's Central Committee in August 1924, in connexion with a curious situation that had arisen in Russian industry. According to a statistical calculation, the correctness of which was not generally accepted, industrial wages had risen by 90 per cent between October 1922 and January 1924. During the same period output per man-day had risen only by 23 per cent. As, in consequence of the civil war, the standard of living of the Russian workers had been depressed far below any essential minimum, the Central Committee put up with this disproportion between the rise of wages and improvement in industrial efficiency. But with the evident, if still incomplete, normalization of the economy, this state of affairs could not continue. Henceforth, it was stated, productivity of labour must rise quicker than wages.

It is not possible to make any precise comparison between the trends in wages and industrial efficiency during subsequent years. The official statistical indices were not very reliable and were hotly disputed. In the middle twenties the Trotskyist opposition asserted that, while the Government claimed that industrial wages had risen to the pre-war level, real wages were actually less than two-thirds of what they had been before 1914. The opposition concluded that the wages policy of 1924 should be reversed, and that wages should be increased at least at the same rate at which productivity of labour was rising. Against this, the official spokesmen advanced the argument, which has since become something of an axiom, that, if industry was to expand, productivity of labour must rise more quickly than wages so as to create a sufficiently wide margin of resources for capital investment.[1]

The entire wages policy of the pre-war Plans was based on this principle, which did not, of course, meet with any open criticism or opposition on the part of the trade unions. The sixteenth party conference, when it launched the first Five-Year Plan, foreshadowed an overall rise in the productivity of industrial labour by 110 per cent. Wages were to rise by 71 per cent over the same five-year period.[2] In 1930 alone the increase in productivity was planned to be 25 per cent, while the rise in nominal wages was to amount to 9 per cent and in real wages to 12 per cent. Similar proportions were characteristic for all pre-war Plans. The first post-war Five-Year Plan, however, provided for an increase in wages

[1] The validity of this argument is, of course, relative only. Whether an increase in wages corresponding to the rise in industrial efficiency is compatible with a large expansion in capital investment depends on a great variety of specific circumstances. Very often the two things are not incompatible. Any rise in efficiency of labour is normally expressed in the additional output of a given factory, industry, or of the national industry as a whole. A given capital outlay which used to produce 100 units may, because of the rise in efficiency, produce, say, 120, 20 per cent more. Wages form only part of the capital outlay. An increase in wages by 20 per cent need not necessarily absorb the major part of the additional product. In Russian industry in the middle twenties wages amounted to slightly more than 50 per cent of the total cost of production. The annual increase in industrial output was in fact of the order of 20 per cent in every year from 1926 to 1929. A 20 per cent increase in wages would have left about half of the value of the additional product for new investment. In the late thirties wages were only 25 per cent of the total cost of production in Russian industry. This reflected the change in the 'organic structure of capital' due to modernization and expansion of plant. At this more advanced stage an annual 20 per cent increase in wages, assuming a 20 per cent increase in the gross industrial output, should, *ceteris paribus*, still have left as much as three-quarters of the value of the additional product for new investment. While rises in wages keeping pace with rises in efficiency may slow down capital expansion in some cases, this does not seem to be the rule in Russian or in any other industry. (For the data given here see Kuibyshev's speech in *8. Syezd Profsoyuzov*, p. 373 and *Bolshaya Sovetskaya Entsiklopediya, SSSR* (Moscow, 1948), p. 1096.)

[2] *V.K.P. (b) o Profsoyuzakh*, pp. 393–5.

by 48 per cent and in productivity by only 36 per cent above the 1940 levels.

The size of the national wages bill was and still is as strictly planned as were the targets of output, the rates of capital investment, the proportions of expansion between heavy and light industry, and so on. Theoretically, the planned wages bill represents only another name for the mass of consumer goods which the Plan allocates to the industrial population—this is the *real* wages bill. An increase in the national wages bill without a corresponding increase in the volume of consumer goods must, of course, lead to inflation. The Soviet trade unions understood and accepted this maxim from their earliest years—they had learnt their lesson from the depreciation of the rouble in the First World War, during the revolution, the civil war, and the early twenties. As, under the Five-Year Plans, the output of consumer industries was rigidly fixed in advance, the trade unions were left with no scope for bargaining over the national wages bill, even if they had wanted to bargain.

This statement needs perhaps to be qualified. In theory, the trade unions exercise their influence at the very top of the governmental pyramid, at the stage when the Polit-bureau, the Government, and the planning authorities still discuss the main features of any Five-Year Plan. It is impossible to say whether or to what extent they have ever pressed for higher wages (that is, for an increase in the targets of output set for consumer industries) before any plan has been accepted. We do not know, in other words, to what extent the trade unions have ever acted as a pressure group on the highest level of the administration. What is certain is that they could not act as pressure groups or bargain at the medium and lower levels. Once the national plan had been adopted and broken down into regional plans the trade unions could not and would not ask for any revision of those of its features which dealt with wages and conditions of labour. No trade unionist would take upon himself the odium of trying to upset the plan.

This is not to say that wages policy has always worked smoothly and efficiently, 'according to plan'. We have seen how the fluidity of labour threatened to disturb the working of the planned economy. Other spontaneous reactions on the part of this or that section of the population to certain features of governmental policy had similar upsetting effects. The entire wages policy of the first Five-Year Plan, for instance, was based on an anticipation of a cheapening of consumer goods. Hence the rises in nominal wages were as a rule planned to be lower than those in real wages. (For instance, in 1930 nominal wages were to rise by 9 per cent and real wages by 12.) This anticipation did not come true. The revolt of vast sections of the peasantry against collectivization, the mass slaughter of cattle, and the resulting scarcity of goods caused a steep rise in the prices of nearly all un-rationed goods and often made it impossible for the Government to supply the rationed goods. Thus, whatever the rise in the nominal wages, real wages went down, although it is not easy to say by just how much. The fact is that through-out the first Five-Year Plan the 'scissors' between the ever-rising nominal wages and the declining real wages grew ever wider. The gap was considerably narrowed in the second and third Five-Year Plans, when the supply of food and other consumer goods became more abundant.

So far we have seen how the *national* wages bill has been related to *national* efficiency. The next step was to correlate *individual* wages and *individual* efficiency.

Before the period of planned economy, in the twenties, two major reforms of wages policy had been carried out. The first, based on resolutions of the fourth Congress of the Trade Unions, took place in 1921–2. The scale of wages then introduced comprised seventeen grades, nine for manual workers and eight for clerical employees. The proportion of the lowest to the highest wage was 1 to 3·5. The main differentiation was between the two broad categories of skilled and unskilled labour. The differences in wage rates paid for various grades of skill were relatively slight; and additional rewards showed a decreasing progression in the higher grades. Thus, for instance, while a man in the third grade of skill earned 25 per cent more than one in the second grade, the worker of the eighth category earned only 10·5 per cent more than his colleague in the seventh grade. This decreasing scale of additional rewards is now retrospectively denounced as a manifestation of *uravnilovka*, the condemned egalitarian heresy. Yet throughout the twenties this scale of wages was considered to be an excess of bourgeois inequality surviving in the proletarian State. The leadership of the trade unions was on this ground denounced as the mouthpiece of a new labour aristocracy by the Trotskyist opposition; and it met the opposition's criticisms with shamefaced embarrassment, admitting that the differences in wages were too great and ought to be reduced. At the seventh Congress of the Trade Unions, in December 1926, Tomsky, then still an all-powerful member of the Politbureau, on the one hand opposed the demands of his critics for a general rise in wages but, on the other, conceded the need for equalization.[1] In the middle twenties the discrepancies in wages were in fact slightly reduced.[2]

[1] *7. Syezd Profsoyuzov*, p. 49 and passim. Tomsky told the Congress that well-wishing foreign visitors had been shocked by the differences between the earnings of skilled and unskilled workers in Russia. At that time such criticisms coming from foreign visitors, mostly Communists, still made their impression on the Russian Communist Party.

[2] See Dogadov's statement in *8. Syezd Profsoyuzov*, p. 87. In 1926 the highest wage paid, say, in railway workshops, was only 53 per cent above the lowest, while in engineering the highest wage was 128 per cent above the lowest.

The second tariff reform, carried out in 1927–8, was calculated to give further satisfaction to the demand for more equality. Gradations between the earnings of the skilled and unskilled workers were lessened. 'The higher the tariff grade of the worker the smaller was his additional reward', says a recent critic of the reform. An attempt was also made to limit the application of piece-rates.

It is interesting to note that the egalitarian trend found a consistent and early critic in Stalin himself who already in 1925 admonished the fourteenth Congress of the party: 'We must not play with the phrase about equality. This is playing with fire.'[1] But a drastic practical reaction against the egalitarian trend was initiated by Stalin only in the middle of 1931, in one of his famous speeches to industrial managers. 'In a number of enterprises', Stalin then said, 'the wage rates have been fixed in such a way that there is almost no difference between skilled and unskilled labour, between heavy and light labour. This levelling causes the unskilled worker to be disinterested in the acquisition of skill.'[2] He blamed the fluidity of labour on the 1927–8 wage scales, saying that there would have been little of it if workers had been given the chance to improve their skills and raise their wages by staying in their jobs.

Soon afterwards the national wage structure was radically remade. A many-sided differentiation of wage rates was introduced, as between entire industries, geographical regions, and categories of skill. The differentiation as between industries was calculated to promote heavy industry. Thus, coal-miners, who under the old scale held the fourteenth place with regard to rates, were promoted to the fourth place in 1935, and to the second in 1937. Oil workers moved from the eighth to the first place; iron and steel workers from

[1] J. Stalin, *Sochinenia* (Moscow, in progress), vii, 376.
[2] J. Stalin, *Voprosy Leninizma* (Problems of Leninism) 11th ed., p. 334.

the ninth to the fifth, and so on. The light industries were put at the bottom of the scale. Geographical differentiation of wages was designed to encourage the migration of workers to new industrial centres in the Urals and beyond, where they could get higher wages than elsewhere. In this way the wages policy was turned into a direct instrument of national policy aiming at the development of heavy industry and the industrialization of the eastern provinces.[1] The nationally planned demand for certain categories of goods led to a deliberate raising of wages in the industries producing those goods. Planning thus performed 'in an organized manner' the function which the mechanism of wages performed 'blindly and spontaneously' in a *laissez-faire* economy, where, too, the demand for goods co-determined the level of wages and its fluctuations.

The central feature of the reform initiated in 1931 consisted, however, in the differentiation of individual wages. It is significant that since that reform no comprehensive statistics of wages have been published, except for claims about periodic rises in the national bill of nominal wages and in the average wage, claims which cannot be translated into terms of real wages because the publication of price indices has also been discontinued. In the total of the national wages bill the earnings of industrial workers and of office employees are lumped together. The distribution of incomes between these two categories has not been disclosed. The withholding of these statistical data from publication is primarily a matter of social policy; although the regime has openly conducted a systematic campaign against 'levellers', a frank disclosure of the real differences between the earnings of various categories of workers and employees would almost certainly have

[1] In June 1931 the Railwaymen's Trade Union was ordered to work out, in co-operation with the Commissariat of Transport, special wage rates for railwaymen employed on the eastern and far northern lines (*V.K.P.* (*b*) *o Profsoyuzakh*, pp. 534–51).

caused considerable ideological embarrassment—it would show how far the pendulum had now swung in the direction of inequality.

Another guiding principle of the new policy was to extend piece-work to as wide a field of industry as possible. This met with some opposition, ineffective, of course, in the trade unions, already purged from Trotskyist and Tomskyist elements. Even the Commissariat of Labour had its hesitations; and its organ *Voprosy Truda* stated that 'the development of technique, the increasing role of transport and electricity . . . narrow the field of industry where piece rates are applicable'.[1] Through a number of instructions from the Central Committee of the party the new policy was, however, enforced. Thus, a resolution of 7 July 1931 instructed the Central Committee of the Miners' Trade Union and the managers of the coal mines of the Donetz to do away 'within two months' with the equalization of wages and to transfer 85 to 90 per cent of the underground staffs and 70 per cent of all other workers to piece-rates. The trade unions were rudely reminded that they had merely a consultative voice in fixing new wage scales: the same instruction stated that the Norms and Conflicts Commissions (RKK), which were to fix the new rates, should be placed under the leadership of the pit managers. Similar instructions were issued to every major branch of industry with the result that, whereas before the reform 57 per cent of the total of man-hours worked were paid in piece-rates, the percentage of man-hours so paid rose to 75 in 1937.[2]

Simple piece-rates were, however, not considered to be powerful enough as incentives to higher production; and so-called progressive rates were introduced. Simple—that is,

[1] Quoted from *Pravda* of 7 July 1931 which attacked the Commissariat of Labour for this statement.
[2] *Bolshaya Sovetskaya Entsiklopediya, SSSR*, p. 1117.

equal—piece-rates were paid for output up to fixed norms. Output above the norms was paid according to a new scale of rates increasing with the output. Thus an instruction of 29 March 1940 on wages in the Donetz coal mines, signed by Stalin and Molotov, ordered, apart from a 100 per cent increase in normal rates for coal-getters, the following progressive piece-rates: a coal-getter who produced 10 per cent more than his norm received double the normal rate for output above the norm. One who produced, say, 20 per cent above the norm was paid treble rates for output above the norm.[1] Where the introduction of piece-rates was technically impossible, time bonuses served to stimulate intensity of labour. 'Brigade piece-rates' were a special form of payment introduced in industries where the output of the individual worker could not be measured in piece-rates but the output of a whole team lent itself to such measurement. The total output of the team was paid in piece-rates; and then the members of the team divided the collective wage among themselves according to their qualifications and the time worked by every member. This form of payment was not encouraged, however, because it was found that the teams of workers showed a 'deplorable' bias towards egalitarianism.[2]

The eventual result of these many-sided and thorough-

[1] *V.K.P. (b) o Profsoyuzakh*, pp. 654–65. John Scott in his *Behind the Urals* (London, Secker & Warburg, 1942, p. 117) gives the following scale of progressive rates for metal workers in Magnitogorsk in the middle thirties:

Production in Percentages of the Plan per Month	Payment in Percentages of Basic Rates First Group	Second Group
less than 100	75	75
100	100	100
101–120	130	120
121–130	170	150
131–150	200	180
151 and upwards	300	250

To the first group belonged the highly skilled technical personnel, while the second comprised foremen and skilled personnel of a lower category.
[2] *Bolshaya Sovetskaya Entsiklopediya, SSSR*, p. 1115.

going changes in the national structure of wages, carried out through the trade unions, can be seen from the following figures: on 1 January 1938 43 per cent of all Soviet workers and employees were paid simple piece-rates. Progressive piece-rates were received by 32 per cent. Of the 25 per cent who were still paid time-rates, 9 per cent received bonuses in addition to their basic wages. Only 16 per cent of all workers and employees continued to receive old-fashioned, ordinary time-wages.

(e) *Stakhanovism*. 'Socialist emulation' thus became uninhibited competition between individual workers for higher output and higher wages. The trade unions spurred on that competition. In the early thirties the form of emulation they favoured was *udarnichestvo* or shock-work. Since 1935 Stakhanovism has taken its place.

The difference between the two 'movements' is one of degree. The emulation in output associated with the Stakhanov method has been more intense and brutal than the older system of shock-work. It has also spread over a wider field of industry. It was with the development of Stakhanovism that the differentiation of wages was greatly intensified and made common.

The transition from the one method to the other was connected primarily with the abolition of food rationing in 1934 and with the Government's attempt to stabilize the rouble. In the first years of the planned economy, up to 1934, money wages were of little significance, because the rouble had been depreciated. The industrial system was based mainly on wages in kind; and the differentiation of wages expressed itself, as under military communism, primarily in a differential rationing system. This included various categories of canteens, restaurants, and shops for the various categories of workers. The differences between the nominal piece-rates were not very great. High rates paid in worthless currency were poor incentives to higher production. The shock-worker was not interested in saving money for future purchases. All this changed at a stroke with the abolition of rationing and the stabilization of the rouble. The nominal piece-rates acquired real value; and the progressively growing rates paid for output above norm represented steep increases in the purchasing power of the worker who had earned them.

The scope for differentiation of wages now became incomparably wider than hitherto. As long as wages in kind predominated it was very difficult to give different rations to unskilled and semi-skilled workers, or to devise any elastic system of rewards for various categories of skilled workers. A differential rationing system may comprise five, six, or, at the most, seven categories of rations; the gradations in skill and productivity are much more numerous—no rationing system can do full justice to their subtlety and variety.

Even differential rationing has, therefore, a faint flavour of *uravnilovka*, the egalitarian heresy, while the piece-wage paid in stable money is completely free from it. To quote Karl Marx: 'Since the quality and intensity of the work are here controlled by the form of the wage itself',[1] the piece-wage automatically registers the slightest difference in the quality and intensity of the work performed. '. . . the wider scope that piece wages gives to individuality', Marx goes on to say, 'tends to develop on the one hand that individuality, and with it the sense of liberty, independence and self-control of the labourers, on the other their competition one with another. Piece work has, therefore, a tendency, while raising individual wages above the average, to lower this average itself. . . Piece wages is the form of wages most in harmony with the capitalist mode of production.'[2] Marx held that the 'sense of liberty and independence' which piece-work gave to the workers was largely illusory—the competition between them was more real. This, however,

[1] Karl Marx, *Capital*.   [2] ibid.

has not prevented the Soviet Government and the Soviet trade unions from hailing piece-wages as the form of payment most in harmony with the socialist mode of production. It is in Stakhanovism that the piece-wage has achieved its supreme triumph.

The origin of that 'movement' goes back to a production record achieved by a coal-getter named Alexei Stakhanov, who was reported to have produced 102 tons of coal in one shift, fourteen times as much as the norm, on 31 August 1935. The limelight of trade union propaganda was at once turned upon him. Workers all over the country were called on to imitate him. The fact, however, that Stakhanov gave his name to this 'movement' was as much accidental as the 'movement' itself was carefully staged.

The actual achievements of Stakhanovism have been the subject of much controversy. While Soviet propagandists have proclaimed Stakhanovism to be a peculiar feature of socialist organization of labour, many critics have dismissed it as sheer bluff. As far as one can judge from Soviet reports and eye-witness accounts of independent foreigners, Stakhanovism has greatly helped to raise industrial efficiency from the extremely low level at which it stood when the experiment was started. It seems that the Central Committee of the party was essentially right when, in December 1935, it stated that:

The Stakhanov movement signifies a new organization of labour, the rationalization of technological processes, the correct distribution of labour in production, the freeing of skilled workers from second-rate preparatory work, the better organization of work sites, the securing of the rapid increase of labour productivity and of a considerable growth in the wages and salaries of workers and employees.[1]

This statement implicitly explains how the production records were achieved and it also allows us to distinguish between the startling façade of Stakhanovism and the

[1] *V.K.P.* (*b*) *o Profsoyuzakh*, p. 579.

reality behind it. By the middle thirties, it will be remembered, the technical equipment of Russian industry had been
modernized and greatly expanded. Yet, because of obsolete
methods of work and extreme shortage of industrial skill,
the coefficient of utilization of the new equipment was still
extremely low. Moderate improvements in the organization
of labour were able to yield and did yield quite abnormal,
spectacular rises in productivity. This was the indubitably
progressive facet of Stakhanovism. The records of individuals
were usually followed by a general raising of the average
norms of output, endorsed by the trade unions; and the new
norms were fixed halfway between the old ones and the
Stakhanovite records. [1]

In part, however, the production records claimed were
publicity stunts. The old norms of output made allowance
for the time which the worker spent on the maintenance of
his tools, on the preparation of the work site, and other
auxiliary functions. The Stakhanovite was as a rule freed
from all auxiliary work, which other people had to do for
him so that he might concentrate on the actual output. This
was, of course, part of the 'correct distribution of labour',
which demanded that the skilled worker should not waste
his time on jobs requiring no skill. But the final production
record resulted most often from the work of a whole team
and not of the individual Stakhanovite, who as a rule claimed
it for himself.

It is often asked just how great has been the inequality

[1] The new norms were fixed by industrial managers and technicians
to the exclusion of the factory committees and the trade unions who now
acted as mere publicity agents for Stakhanovism (ibid. pp. 581, 583–8 and
passim). This can be seen, *inter alia*, from the instructions of the Central
Committee of the party, issued in December 1935, about the revision of
norms that was to be carried out in all industries in 1936. The instructions
contained detailed descriptions of production conferences called for this
purpose. In every case the participants mentioned were only 'managers,
chief engineers, shop managers, foremen and prominent Stakhanovites'—
no representatives of trade unions or factory committees were included.

to which Stakhanovism has led. How does that inequality
compare with differences in incomes in other countries? Only
a very general answer to these questions can be given, because of the fragmentary character of the information available. In spite of the sustained campaign against 'levellers',
which has been going on since 1931, the inequality of incomes in the Soviet Union has hardly achieved anything
like the discrepancy between the incomes of, say, big share-
holders and unskilled labourers in any other country.
Briefly, the inequality *between classes* is less than elsewhere.
But the inequality *inside* the working class, between various
groups of workers, has certainly been much greater than in
any other country. This contention can be illustrated by the
following data given by *Pravda* towards the end of 1935,
shortly after Stakhanovism had been launched. An ordinary
non-Stakhanovite coal-miner doing auxiliary work underground earned 170 roubles per month. The wage of a non-
Stakhanovite coal-getter was 400–500 roubles. The monthly
earnings of a Stakhanovite were more than 1,600 roubles.[1]
It will be interesting to compare these figures with data
obtained in 1948 by a delegation of foreign trade unionists
on a visit to Russia. Thus in 1948 the basic pay of a coal-
getter amounted to as much as 2,000 roubles per month, that
of an auxiliary above-ground worker was 250 roubles, one-
eighth of the coal-getter's wage. Since the early thirties
wages policy in the coal industry has fluctuated, now reducing the discrepancy and now widening it even more; but on
balance the trend has been towards more and not less
inequality. In 1948 there were twelve categories of wages in
the iron and steel industry, eight in machine building, but
only six in industries producing consumer goods. In addition
to higher wages Stakhanovites enjoy important privileges:
free sojourns in rest homes and sanatoria owned by the trade

[1] *Pravda*, 16 November 1935.

unions; the right to have home tutors for their children without payment, free medical help at the Stakhanovite's home, and a number of other services which have raised the Stakhanovite's standard of living far above that of the ordinary worker.[1] Stakhanovism has made of Russia an almost classical country of a labour aristocracy; and the trade unions, in so far as they play any role as a labour organization, have been converted into strongholds of that workers' aristocracy.

In its first years Stakhanovism met with considerable resistance on the part of the lower ranks of trade union officials, who willynilly became the mouthpieces of discontent among the rank and file. This opposition could not become vocal, but it was widespread, intense, and, for a time, dangerously effective.

This is not to say that the workers' reaction to Stakhanovism was uniformly or even predominantly hostile. It was mixed. Some sections of the working class received with satisfaction the opportunity of improving their lot through better and more diligent work. The appeal to the worker's individualism was especially effective because an inherited peasant individualism was still strong in the Soviet working class.[2] But, as in any competitive system, so in Stakhanovism the number of those who were beaten at the competition was greater than the number of those who benefited from it. Those who suffered from Stakhanovite methods were, of course, opposed to them, and they were branded as 'backward elements' by their own trade unions. No doubt there was no lack of such 'backward elements' opposed to technical innovations and rational organization of labour. But among

[1] *Trud*, 1 and 2 November 1935.
[2] The biographies of Stakhanov himself and of other celebrated Stakhanovites are highly instructive. Most Stakhanovites were young workers in their twenties or early thirties who had left the countryside only a few years before.

the discontented were also workers whom ill-health or age had made unfit for the exertion now required to earn a minimum wage. Among those opposed to Stakhanovism was the cadre of industrial workers who had been brought up in class consciousness and class solidarity and taught to regard equality as the ultimate goal of socialism—the good Communists of the preceding era, now denounced as 'petty bourgeois' levellers. This last category of workers was strongly represented among the lower and middle officials of the trade unions.

The opposition to Stakhanovism, with all the mixed motives behind it, formed the background to the violent campaigns against 'saboteurs and wreckers' which were conducted in the middle thirties. Press reports in 1935 and 1936, abounding in much realistic detail and circumstantial evidence, offered some insight into the character of that 'sabotage'. Contrary to later claims, made during the famous purge trials of the old Bolshevik guard, these reports presented the 'wrecking' and 'sabotage' not as the result of any political plot, but as the spontaneous and, at times, Luddite-like resistance of workers to new methods of labour. Attacks by workers on Stakhanovites, attempts to intimidate them and prevent them from assisting the industrial managers in raising average norms of output, occurred quite frequently. Lower trade union officials were sometimes implicated in such attempts.[1] In some cases Stakhanovites were assassinated. Much more often workers damaged, put out of order, or concealed the Stakhanovite's tools so as to disorganize or delay his work.

The party's reaction to this resistance was determined but not immediately effective. 'In some enterprises', so Zhdanov stated in November 1935, 'the Stakhanov move-

[1] *Trud*, 3 November 1935.

ment has met with resistance. . . The party will not shrink from any measures that will help it to sweep away all the resisters from the victorious path of the Stakhanovite movement.'[1] But in the following year and even the year after innumerable resolutions acknowledged the continuance of the opposition to Stakhanovism and the ambiguous attitude of the trade unions on the spot. A typical resolution of April 1937, signed by Stalin and Molotov, asserted that previous instructions on Stakhanovism had not been obeyed, that differential wage rates had not been introduced, and that trade unions and even party committees had refused to expose 'wreckers'.[2] Nevertheless, Zhdanov's threat that the 'party will sweep away all the resisters' was eventually carried out. During the great purges of 1937–8 the trade unions were among the chief victims. After the purges were over, in March 1939, Shvernik announced at the eighteenth Congress of the party that 'the composition of the Trade Union committees in factories and other establishments was changed to the extent of 70–80 per cent and of the central committees to the extent of 96 per cent'.[3] The opposition to Stakhanovism seems to have been largely overcome since then, and Stakhanovism, that mixture of progressive rationalization and old-time sweated labour, has come to be accepted as the peculiarly Soviet style of labour.

(*f*) *Trade Unions and Social Insurance.* As the trade unions, unable or unwilling to defend the workers, tended to become merely vestigial institutions, new functions were transferred to them, presumably in order to justify their continued existence. In 1933 the Commissariat of Labour was officially abolished and its functions and funds were transferred to the trade unions. The main consequence of this reform was that

[1] *Pravda,* 13 November 1935.   [2] *V.K.P. (b) o Profsoyuzakh,* pp. 590–3.
[3] See his statement in *The Land of Socialism* (Moscow, Foreign Languages Publishing House, 1939), p. 405.

the trade unions were charged with the administration of social insurance.[1] The Department of Social Insurance in the Central Council of Trade Unions was the body directly responsible for this new and vast field of work and for the utilization of social insurance funds. Branches of that department were set up at every level of the trade union machinery. Every factory committee formed its council for social insurance; and at the lowest level special insurance delegates were attached to every shop committee. In 1948 altogether about one million active trade unionists performed the functions of insurance delegates. Their task has been to regulate locally all matters concerning invalid pensions, sickness benefits, etc. The trade unions also took over the management of holiday resorts, sanatoria, and rest homes. Before the Second World War they owned 853 sanatoria and rest homes capable of accommodating 161,000 persons. Many of these establishments were destroyed during the Nazi invasion. The present Five-Year Plan provides for their reconstruction and expansion—in 1950 the sanatoria and rest homes should be able to accommodate 185,000 persons.

This transformation of the trade unions into a social insurance organization has had its undoubted advantages. It has given a very broad basis to the entire system of social insurance. The voluntary unpaid work of one million insurance delegates in factories and workshops must have lowered the cost of social insurance and brought its administration closer to the working masses. On the other hand, the entire system of the social services has been used as an instrument for raising the productivity of labour. We have seen how the rates of sickness benefits and invalid pensions were graded so as to serve that purpose. The number of sanatoria,

[1] The trade unions thereby came into possession of very considerable assets. The funds of social insurance amounted to 10·4 milliard roubles under the first Five-Year Plan and to 32·5 milliard under the second. They amount to 61·6 milliard roubles under the post-war Five-Year Plan.

117

rest homes, and similar establishments has been rather limited in relation to needs, and so practically they have been accessible in the main only to the high administrative and technical personnel and to Stakhanovites.

These two purposes of the 1933 reform, that of giving the system of social insurance a broad unbureaucratic base in the trade unions and that of harnessing the entire system to the Government's economic policy, have not always been compatible. The insurance delegates in the factories were not always inclined to give the Stakhanovites priority in the benefits and the facilities which they, the insurance delegates, administered. Here, too, the Government, assisted by the Central Council of Trade Unions, waged a stubborn fight against the instinctive egalitarianism of rank and file trade unionists. In April 1939 the seventh plenary session of the Central Council of Trade Unions adopted the following characteristic resolution:

The most important means towards strengthening labour discipline has been the improvement in the functioning of state social insurance and the elimination of abuses in that field. Yet many factories and local committees have offended against the decision of the government, the Central Committee of the Party and the Central Council of Trade Unions . . . by the incorrect allocation of relief for temporarily incapacitated workers. . . The factory committees have not paid attention to the entries in the labour cards, on the basis of which they should ascertain how long the applicant for relief has been permanently employed at a given factory or institution. The plenary session condemns these anti-state activities of the factory and local committees which offend against the decision of 28 December 1938, fixing the rates of relief under the social insurance scheme.

The central committees of the Trade Unions are hereby reminded of their duty to improve the work of the councils and commissions of social insurance, to establish permanent control over the correctness of the allocation and payment of allowances to temporarily incapacitated workers and to charge with responsibility those guilty of offending against the scales of allowances fixed by the government, the Central Committee of the Party and the Central Council of the Trade Unions. . .

The Praesidium of the Central Council of Trade Unions is instructed to consult the People's Commissar for Health of the U.S.S.R. about further improvements in medical services for workers and employees and about the measures that are being taken by the People's Commissar for Health against doctors who admit idlers and malingerers to hospitals.[1]

Since 1933 the trade unions have also been responsible for protection of labour. The central committees of the trade unions maintain technical inspectorates which employ several thousand full-time industrial inspectors. In addition, part-time voluntary workers act as inspectors in factories and shops. They check, at least in precept, how the industrial managements utilize governmental funds allocated for labour protection.[2] The manner in which these funds are to be used is the subject of special agreements periodically concluded between industrial managements and factory committees. At the lowest level, in the shops, one worker in every group of trade unionists is the inspector responsible for protection of female and juvenile labour and for observing the length of the working day,[3] for arranging holidays, etc.

The trade unions have also been made responsible for welfare and a number of auxiliary functions designed to improve the workers' standard of living within the limits set by the Plan and the fixed fund of wages. It is in these fields that the unions have found some compensation for the loss of their bargaining power over wages. Since the grave food crises of the early thirties it has been a common practice of Soviet factories to develop their own auxiliary farms and vegetable gardens. This practice was further developed during the Second World War, and it then helped to keep the industrial population supplied with food. The trade unions have assisted

[1] See Appendix in N. Shvernik, *O Rabote Profsoyuzov v Svyazi s Resheniyami XVIII Syezda V.K.P. (b)* (Trade Union Activities in connexion with the Decisions taken by the Eighteenth Congress of the All-Union Communist Party; Moscow, 1939), pp. 90–1.

[2] In the current Five-Year Plan about 5 milliard roubles have been allocated for labour protection.

[3] The working day was seven hours before the war and was raised to eight in 1940.

in the organization and running of the auxiliary farms. They have also controlled the work of the so-called Workers' Supply Departments, factory canteens and co-operative shops. One of many characteristic resolutions states, for instance, that the chairman of any factory committee (that is, the chief trade union organizer on the spot) is personally responsible for any malpractices in the co-operatives and food supply centres. 'The Trade Union officials who carry out this control ought to have some knowledge of bookkeeping and to be able to analyse the calculation of prices so as to know how and where malpractices occur.'[1] Similarly, the trade unions check how funds allocated for housing of workers are used, what is the quality of the houses built, and so on. Since the Second World War letters and articles by trade unionists have frequently appeared in the press censuring industrial managers and even ministers for neglecting to carry out housing programmes.

Finally, the trade unions have taken an active part in *Osoaviakhim* and other paramilitary organizations; and the very strong sports organizations of the trade unions have been useful auxiliaries of the Armed Forces.[2]

---

[1] *V.K.P. (b) o Profsoyuzakh*, p. 577.
[2] It is claimed, for instance, that in the Second World War the trade unions trained two million skiers for the Red Army.

5
Machinery and Organization of Trade Unions

THE organization of the trade unions has undergone many changes since the revolution. The second Congress of the Trade Unions adopted the 'production principle', which required that all workers and employees of any enterprise, regardless of their craft or trade, should be members of the same union. The workers and employees, say, of an engineering plant, no matter what their individual occupation, joined the trade union of the metal workers. The seventh Trade Union Congress (1926) adopted the rule 'one economic organ—one union'. This was designed to adjust the structure of the trade unions to that of the economic administration so that one commissariat should as far as possible deal with only one union, and *vice versa*.[1] Subsequently the number and organization of trade unions varied in accordance with changes and reforms in the economic administration. In 1930 there existed only 23 national trade unions. Since then their number has steadily grown with the multiplication of economic commissariats (or, later, of ministries). In 1931 there already existed 45 national trade unions; in 1934—154; in 1939—168; in 1944—176; but in 1949, after several mergers there existed only 67 national trade union organizations.[2]

The membership of the trade unions has steadily grown, with the exception of a short period in the early twenties when there was a considerable decline during the transition from military communism to NEP. A noteworthy feature in the organization of the unions has been the so-called single

[1] *7. Syezd Profsoyuzov*, p. 43.   [2] *Trud*, 23 May 1949

121

membership card: a member of any union, when he changes his occupation, becomes automatically a member of any other union, without paying a new entrance fee. This principle underlines the organic unity of the entire movement and its freedom from sectional or craft divisions.

The accuracy of the membership statistics cannot be ascertained. The following table gives the official claims of membership in various years between 1917 and 1948:

June 1917	1,450,000	1925	6,950,000
January 1918	2,532,000	1926	8,768,000
January 1919	3,639,000	1928	10,995,000
April 1920	4,326,000	1933	17,126,000
July 1921	8,400,000[1]	1940	25,000,000
January 1922	6,700,000	1947	27,000,000
September 1922	5,100,000	1948	28,500,000

In 1918–22, under military communism, membership was 'collective' and compulsory. The workers and employees of any business joined the trade union as a body; and the individual worker or employee had no right to contract out. With the transition to NEP the principle of voluntary and individual membership was adopted, primarily on Lenin's insistence. This caused the spectacular decline in membership in 1921–2, even though the transition to voluntary membership was only gradual. In the twenties the voluntary character of the organization was real enough, although adherence to the trade union did, of course, secure advantages to the worker. In precept, the principle of voluntary organization has been preserved until now. But the material advantages of membership have grown so enormously that one wonders

[1] This was the figure given by Andreev at the fifth Congress of the Trade Unions (5. *Vserossiiskii Syezd Profsoyuzov*, p. 41). *Bolshaya Sovetskaya Entsiklopediya* gives the membership for May 1921 as only 6·5 million, nearly 2 million less than the figure given by Andreev. Similar discrepancies occur between figures for other years as well. Thus the Encyclopaedia claims a membership of more than 9·5 million for 1926, whereas the number given at the fifteenth party conference was less than 8·8 million. See *V.K.P. (b) o Profsoyuzakh*, p. 239.

how it is that only 90 and not 100 per cent of the total number of workers and employees is claimed to belong to the trade unions. It will be remembered that the worker who does not belong to a union receives only 50 per cent of the sickness benefits paid to the trade unionist.

In the early years the trade unions organized almost exclusively the manual workers. As a matter of principle they refused to admit the higher technical personnel, and they were not over-anxious to organize civil servants. Soon after the revolution, professional people and clerical employees were drawn into the movement, and trade unions of teachers and of the 'medical and sanitary personnel' were formed. Later, the higher technical and administrative personnel were also organized, including industrial managers, whose standing in relation to the workers was actually that of employers.[1]

The massive vertical structure of the trade unions rests upon the *fabzavkom* or the factory committee, its basic unit. The factory committees, as we know, aspired to independence from the unions and even tried to act as their rivals in the early days of the revolution.[2] This aspiration was completely

[1] The inclusion of managers in the trade unions was justified by the familiar argument that they, and the economic administration at large, represented the proletarian State and were therefore by definition not opposed to the workers. 'As, in the U.S.S.R.', says the *Great Soviet Encyclopaedia*, 'there do not exist and cannot exist any class antagonisms between workers and economic administrators, and as the parties to any collective agreement are representatives of the same class and pursue the common objectives of developing socialist production and raising the material and cultural level of the toilers, the essential purpose of any collective agreement is at present: to secure the fulfilment and over-fulfilment of production plans, to further higher productivity of labour, to improve the organization of labour and to raise the responsibility of the administration and trade unions for the material and cultural well-being of the workers . . .' (*Bolshaya Sovetskaya Entsiklopediya*, SSSR, p. 1758). This view does not quite tally with Lenin's insistence on the need of the workers to defend themselves against the State, in so far as that State is 'bureaucratically deformed' and is not a proletarian State *tout court*, but a State of workers and peasants. Nor does the view of the perfect harmony between managers and workers explain why collective agreements, if they are not a pure formality, are needed at all.   [2] See p. 17, above.

defeated, and, after a complex evolution lasting nearly two decades, the factory committees took up a position in which they are much closer to the administration and the industrial managements than to the workers.

The factory committee is elected at a general meeting of all trade unionists in any factory, mine, or office. In precept, the general meeting is the sovereign master of the factory committee; in actual fact the committee takes its orders and instructions from the trade union hierarchy, the party, and the management rather than from its electors. In the intervals between the general meetings—according to the rarely observed statutes the factory committees ought to be elected every year—the factory committee represents the trade union on the spot. Its chairman is usually one of the three all-powerful personalities—the *troika*—in any industrial concern—the other two are the manager and the secretary of the party cell.

The factory committee works through the following specialized commissions:

(*a*) The Council of Social Insurance.

(*b*) The Wages Commission.

(*c*) The Commission for Labour Protection.

(*d*) The Commission for Cultural and Educational Activities.

(*e*) The Housing Commission.

(*f*) The Commission for Workers' Supplies.

(*g*) The Commission for Workers' Inventions and Rationalization.

(*h*) The Commission for Gardening and Auxiliary Farming.

(*i*) The Commission for Assistance to Servicemen's Families. [1]

[1] This branch of the factory committee has been in existence only since the Second World War.

Apart from these permanent bodies, temporary commissions may be set up to deal with special tasks. The factory committee also participates in the important RKK (Rastsenochnaya Konfliktnaya Komisya), the Norms and Conflicts Commission, which deals with complaints from workers and managers. The factory committee is represented in the RKK on a basis of parity with the management; but as a rule the manager, or his appointee, presides over the RKK.

Within the limits set by governmental labour policy the functions of the factory committee are manifold and important. During 1948 and 1949 the factory committee concluded collective agreements. But its initiative in this field was limited, because the local collective agreements must be strictly modelled on the central collective agreement concluded for a whole industry between the ministry in charge of that industry and the central committee of the corresponding trade union. The local collective agreement can at best introduce only very minor variations in the general norms of output and productivity, wages, and so on. The role of the factory committee is more important in the fields of labour protection, in providing for industrial safety, and in a large variety of welfare activities.

In most industrial concerns the factory committee is the basic but not the lowest unit of the organization. Below it is the shop committee which is elected in any shop employing at least one hundred workers. The structure of the shop committee is closely modelled on that of the factory committee; nearly all the commissions of the factory committee, listed above, have their counterparts in commissions of the shop committee. The lowest link in the organization is the so-called *Profgrup*, a group of trade unionists consisting of twenty members and usually comprising a brigade or a team of workers employed in a particular sector of the shop. It is through joining the *Profgrup* that the worker usually becomes a member of the trade union. The *Profgrup* elects its own insurance delegate and its own 'inspector' for labour protection, and one or two other functionaries. The organizer of this smallest unit is called the *Profgruporg*; and he represents his team *vis-à-vis* the industrial management and the trade union hierarchy. The organizer is elected at a meeting of the members of the *Profgrup*.

Periodical production meetings are one of the vital functions of the factory committees. At these meetings the fulfilment of the collective agreement by workers and managements should be checked once every three months. Special production meetings are convened from time to time to encourage workers' inventions and projects for rationalization of labour. At such meetings workers are expected to communicate their observations and suggestions about possible improvements in machinery, organization of labour, handling of materials, etc. The observations and suggestions are collected, sifted, and classified by the special commission of the factory committee which deals with such issues. The industrial managers have special funds at their disposal from which premiums are paid to worker-inventors. Like so many ideas in Soviet trade unionism, this imaginative scheme for the accumulation and utilization of the mass inventiveness of producers has in practice often been marred by official routine: at the production meetings the customary long-winded, monotonous speeches, followed by unanimous adoption of official resolutions, have often swamped any business-like discussion of projects for rationalization of labour. Very often, too, the production meetings have been used merely for the whipping up of the crudest forms of competition between the workers.[1]

[1] It has been customary for the production meetings to advance the so-called *Vstrechnyi Promfinplan*. When the administration has put before the workers the targets of output which their particular factory has to reach within a certain period, the workers are then expected to counter

Above the factory committee there are the town, regional, republican, and central committees of the various trade unions, all elected by secret ballot.[1] At the top of the entire organization there is the All-Union Central Council of the Trade Unions. Re-elected at the tenth Congress of the Trade Unions in April 1949, it consisted of 175 members and 57 alternate members. The Central Council in its turn elects a smaller body, the Praesidium, to act as its executive.

As in all Soviet institutions, so in the Soviet trade unions the organization is in theory governed by the principles of democratic centralism which require that all directing bodies be regularly elected in accordance with statutes but that they should, in the intervals between elections, be the real masters of the organization, with a claim to absolute discipline on the part of the membership. In practice, bureaucratic rather than democratic centralism prevails. The power of the centre is practically unlimited, and the statutory provisions about the responsibility of the trade union officials to their electorate are disregarded. This has been strikingly illustrated by the fact that no less than seventeen years elapsed between the ninth Congress of the Trade Unions which took place in 1932 and the tenth Congress convened in April 1949. In violation of all statutory regulations the Central Council of the Trade Unions did not even bother to go through the formal motions of an election over all these years.

---

the official targets by higher ones—these form the 'industrial-financial counterplan' or *Vstrechnyi Promfinplan*.

The factory committees are also supposed to carry out periodical surveys of industrial plant in order to ensure its proper maintenance. See N. Shvernik, *O Rabote Profsoyuzov v Svyazi s Resheniyami XVIII Syezda V.K.P. (b)* pp. 37, 89.

[1] As an exception, insurance delegates and inspectors for labour protection are elected in open ballot.

6

The Tenth Trade Union Congress

I T is not very clear why after an interval of seventeen years a Trade Union Congress was convened in 1949. There had been no apparent reason for this sudden return to half-forgotten 'parliamentary' procedures. Nothing startling happened during the Congress; no new policy was announced; nor was any fresh light shed on the evolution of the trade unions since the Congress of 1932. The chairman of the All-Union Central Council, V. V. Kuznetsov, did not in his report even attempt to review the trends or discuss the changes in Soviet trade unionism between the two Congresses. The newly-adopted statute did not alter the structure of the organization, except in one point to be discussed later. Finally, the election of the new All-Union Central Council brought little or no change in the leadership. The only hypothetical explanation for the calling of the Congress is that the regime may have been anxious to revive, within limits prescribed by the single-party system, some of the formal democratic practices that had been suspended in connexion with the political convulsions of the thirties and the Second World War.

A significant sidelight on the character of the trade union leadership was given in the report of the Mandate Commission on the composition of the Congress. (The *rapporteur* was N. V. Popova.) From this it is clear that the delegates to the Congress represented, to a greater extent than is true of such gatherings outside Russia, the trade union hierarchy rather than the rank and file. Only 23·5 per cent of all delegates were workers. 43 per cent were full-time trade union

officials. 39 per cent were members of the Central Committees of the Trade Unions in control of the sixty-seven national
organizations. 9·4 per cent of the delegates came from the
technical intelligentsia (compared with only 2 per cent at
the previous Congress). 20-odd per cent of the participants, at the most, were trade union officials of medium or
low rank.[1] 85 per cent of all delegates had some governmental award, the distinctive mark of a member of the
'labour aristocracy'. 71 per cent of the delegates had secondary or higher education—only about 20 per cent had
received not more than elementary education. (At the ninth
Congress 60 per cent had only elementary education.) 72
per cent were either members of the Communist Party or
had applied for membership. (A striking feature was the very
active participation of women: nearly 40 per cent of the
delegates were women, compared with only 18 at the previous Congress.)

These data reflect the dominating position held inside the
unions by the officials and the 'labour aristocracy' and also
the higher educational standards attained by these groups
since the early thirties.

Some significance may be attached to one post-war development which was not, however, discussed in any real sense
by the Congress, namely, the resumption of collective agreements between trade unions and industrial managements.
This practice, too, had been discarded since the early thirties.
In February 1933 collective agreements were formally
abolished by governmental decree; but even before that,
under the first Five-Year Plan, they had tended to become
meaningless. What used to be their central feature—the
settlement of wage claims and of conditions of labour—was
directly regulated by the Government. Since 1947, however,
collective agreements have been revived ('on Comrade

[1] *Trud*, 23 April 1949.

129

Stalin's demand', as V. V. Kuznetsov stated at the tenth Congress[1]) in order 'to stimulate the fulfilment and over-fulfilment of the economic plans'. The explanation explains nothing, for the Government must have been equally anxious to 'stimulate the fulfilment of economic plans' in the thirties, when collective agreements were declared to be no longer needed. It can only be surmised that in this instance, too, the Government has been anxious to give its labour policy some democratic appearance, possibly in order to calm a post-war *malaise* in the working class.

The renewal of collective agreements gave rise to a faint controversy in the press over their scope and meaning, but it has been commonly agreed that the contracts are not meant to settle wages and conditions of labour, which continue to be regulated by the Government. Where collective agreements do include clauses on wages such clauses do not embody the results of any collective bargaining; they merely incorporate passages from governmental decrees and instructions.[2] In view of this, the discussion over the meaning of the collective agreements concerned only minor legal points. The 'contracts' nominally impose obligations upon both managements and workers, but such obligations arise out of the economic plan and would have existed no matter whether a collective agreement was concluded or not.[3]

---

[1] *Trud*, 20 April 1949.

[2] 'The present-day collective agreement usually includes norms regulating the remuneration of labour (rate systems, with coefficients and grades, progressive scales, etc.). These norms, however, are not the result of the collective agreement contract. They originate from the appropriate state authorities. The inclusion of such norms in collective agreements is intended . . . to facilitate the mobilization of manual and office workers in campaigns for the plan. . .', states Professor V. M. Dogadov in an article on the subject, the English translation of which appeared in *Soviet Studies* (Oxford, Blackwell, 1949), I, 79–84.

[3] In the article just quoted V. M. Dogadov cites the following excerpt from a collective agreement concluded in an ordnance factory: 'Open hearth furnace no. 5 is to be made automatic . . . capital repairs are to be carried out at electro-furnace no. 1 . . . a school for young workers is to

The total exclusion of wages policy from trade union activity must be held responsible for the strange fact that in the main report to the Congress—the report by V. V. Kuznetsov which covered more than four full pages in *Trud*—only the tiniest paragraph was devoted to wages. The Congress was given not a single piece of information about the structure of wages, their purchasing power, and so on.[1] The resolutions of the Congress were equally uninformative, but they contained the characteristic statement that 'it is necessary henceforth, too, to wage the struggle against *uravnilovka.* . . .', that is, against egalitarian attitudes.[2] Since after all the official anathemas hardly anybody would now have dared to advocate egalitarianism, this statement merely means that the Government regards further differentiation of wages, that is, the further growth of inequality, as necessary and that the trade unions accept this view.

A noteworthy change in the organization of the trade unions, carried out in 1948 (again 'on Comrade Stalin's initiative'), is the formation of provincial, regional, and town councils of trade unions. On these councils sit the representatives of all trade unions of any province or locality. Until 1948 the trade unions were organized almost exclusively along vertical lines. The local and provincial bodies of any union were connected with the higher and lower links in their own hierarchy. No solid horizontal organization existed to co-ordinate the activities of various trade unions on a local

---

be built with accommodation for 600 pupils; a building for a polyclinic serving the workers of the factory is to be built; one five-storey building, three two-storey buildings, and three three-storey buildings with a total living space of 6,000 square metres are to be built and put into use. . .' Other collective agreements do include some provisions about conditions of labour, but only, to quote Dogadov, about 'isolated, individual matters'.

[1] Kuznetsov stated *inter alia* that the value of social insurance and health services amounted to one-third of the national wages bill.

[2] *Trud*, 11 May 1949.

scale. Thus, the coal miners' union in any locality had hardly any stable links with the union of the steel workers or with that of the textile workers in the same place. Its official intercourse was confined to that with other bodies in the national Coal Miners' Union, whose central committee, in its turn, was subordinated to the All-Union Central Council. This scheme of organization was characteristic of the over-centralization of the trade unions. The local and provincial councils now set up have introduced an element of horizontal organization which should allow various trade unions on the spot to concert their activities. This reform, too, seems to have been dictated by a desire to weaken somewhat the rigidity of the vertical organization, or at least to give the rank and file the impression of relaxation.

All these reforms—the convening of the Congress, the revival of collective agreements, and the setting up of local trade union councils—may add up to a degree of democratization, but will hardly affect the functions and character of the organization as a whole. Somewhat more emphasis than usual was placed on internal democracy in the trade unions and also on the right of the worker to lodge complaints against the management. On the other hand, the newly adopted statute fixes the terms for which the various trade union bodies are to be elected in a manner calculated still further to enhance central control over the entire organization.[1] Thus the Central Council of the Trade Unions is elected for four years. The central committee of any trade union is elected for two years only; so are the regional, provincial, and republican councils. Finally, the primary organizations, the factory committees, are elected for one year only. The higher the trade union authority the greater is its statutory stability and therefore also its power over subordinated bodies.

[1] See Appendix.

The reports given at the tenth Congress leave no doubt about the broad scope of trade union activity in the fields of social insurance and welfare. For that activity the trade unions have built up a vast and in many ways highly impressive organization.

At the base of the organization there were in 1949:

(*a*) one million voluntary organizers of trade union groups —*profgruporgi*;

(*b*) more than 1·2 million voluntary insurance delegates and inspectors of labour;[1]

(*c*) more than one million members of the wages commissions;

(*d*) more than two million rank and file trade unionists active in welfare commissions;

(*e*) altogether more than nine million 'activists', i.e. members voluntarily engaged in part-time work for the unions. The number of 'activists' amounts to one-third of the total membership.

In 1948 more than two million production meetings are reported to have taken place, at which four million suggestions for the rationalization of labour were made.

The mass of voluntary unpaid part-time workers has been a highly important characteristic of the unions—it has a strong flavour of that 'production-democracy' which was juxtaposed to political democracy in the debates of the early twenties. 'I cannot imagine', says S. Gorbunov, chairman of a shop committee, in one of many typical utterances on this subject, 'how we, the leaders of a Trade Union, engaged in intensive productive work all day long, could achieve anything without the backing of this broad mass of activists.

---

[1] The All-Union Central Council has five research institutes and twelve laboratories working on improving protection of industrial labour. They are managed by the Department for Protection of Labour of the All-Union Central Council. The central committees of the individual unions, too, have their specialized research institutes and laboratories.

Seven people have been elected to our shop committee, but in their work they have been assisted by 230 activists. About one hundred people are members of the various commissions of the shop committee. We have 26 group organizers, 52 social inspectors and insurance delegates'.[1]

It is largely through this vast mass of 'activists' that the trade unions have been able to assist in the training of new workers—under the present Five-Year Plan nearly fourteen million workers have been undergoing some degree of retraining, while nearly eight million have been receiving full-time training. The scope of the health services and welfare activities was indicated by V. V. Kuznetsov in his statement that the trade unions gave medical services and facilities for rest to two million of their members in 1948.[2]

[1] *Trud,* 19 April 1949.
[2] V. V. Kuznetsov also stated that occupational diseases among Soviet workers were in 1948 10 per cent less than in 1947 and definitely below pre-war.

7

Road to Serfdom?

I N this survey of their development the Soviet trade unions
are seen as an organic part of the social fabric of the
Soviet Union. Only in the context of the broad changes
that have transformed Soviet society in the three decades of
revolution can the role and functions of the trade unions be
understood.

But it is only proper to ask what, if any, moral of international significance can be drawn from this survey. One
conclusion frequently drawn is that in a planned economy
there is little or no scope for normal trade union activity,
especially for the defence of the workers' interests against the
employer-State. Most admirers of the Soviet Union as well as
its opponents seem to agree on this. In addition, the opponents of planned economy and socialism will see in the story
of the Soviet trade unions a confirmation of their view that
public ownership and economic planning drive the nations
that have opted for these forms of social organization, or
upon whom these forms have been imposed, along the 'road
to serfdom'.

At first sight, the story of the Soviet trade unions appears
to justify such a conclusion. The Soviet trade unions have
often been used by the employer-State as an instrument of
coercion against the working classes. As the organization
designed to forge the workers' solidarity in their struggle for
better living conditions, they have suffered complete atrophy.
As bodies entrusted with the management of social insurance,
and as welfare institutions they have certainly performed and
are still performing very useful services; but these, whatever

the official Soviet theory may be, they have performed as subsidiaries of the State administration, not as autonomous social bodies or working class organizations in the accepted sense.

Yet, on closer analysis, the story of the Soviet trade unions does not really prove the case of the critics of planned economy. For what emerges from this survey is that the peculiar role which the Soviet unions have come to play has been conditioned not by the needs of planned economy as such but by the application of planning to an extremely low level of economic and cultural development, the level at which Russia stood until recently.

The essential condition in which planning can yield the fruits expected from it by its socialist adherents is that it should be applied to an economy of plenty and not to one of scarcity. All socialist advocates of planning, including the Bolsheviks, once used to argue that planned socialist economy could effectively begin only from roughly that level of industrial and cultural development which the older capitalist nations had already attained. At that level, it was argued, planning is both necessary and possible. It is *necessary*—in order to protect society from the wastefulness and moral degradation that result from recurring slumps, mass unemployment, social tension, mass neuroses, and military conflicts. It is *possible*, because the high output of material goods, and the accumulation of industrial-administrative skill and experience and, last but not least, of civilized habits of life enable society to advance in a civilized manner towards economic equality and rational social organization. When the experiment in planned economy was begun, Russia was, and up to a point still is, far below the level at which such results could be expected.

The function of the Russian planned economy was primarily to carry out an industrial revolution such as the older

capitalist countries had gone through long ago. This industrial revolution which elsewhere, either under the *laissez-
faire* system or under bourgeois protectionism, extended over
the life-time of several generations, was in Russia compressed
within little more than one decade, the last before the Second
World War. Within that decade were also compressed all the
horrors that attended earlier industrial revolutions. In a
nation whose large-scale industry produced only 3–4 million
tons of steel and only 30 million pairs of shoes for a population
to 150 million (to take only two striking indices of Russian
poverty towards the end of the twenties) no real movement
towards equality, promised by the revolution, could take
place. In a nation which had accumulated less industrial and
administrative skill and experience than had any medium-
sized European country, in a nation, furthermore, burdened
with the oppressive traditions of inefficient autocracy at its top
and of illiteracy and a barbarous way of life below, the arrears
in economic and cultural development were so enormous,
and the lack of civic responsibility in rulers and ruled alike
was so baffling that the techniques of economic planning
could be developed only in the crudest and most ruthless
forms. This basically determined the place of the trade
unions in Soviet labour policy.

It is a tribute to planned economy that, in spite of the
handicaps under which it has been tried out in Russia, it has
enabled that country to become a great industrial power
within so short a time. But it would be erroneous to deduce
from this that the peculiarly Russian features of labour
policy, the features that have in fact more than a flavour
of revived serfdom about them, are inherent in planned
economy or more specifically in socialist planning. There is
no reason to assume that in any society which already has
at its disposal a more or less modern apparatus for industrial
production and substantial reserves of trained man-power

planned economy would reproduce the worst aspects of the Russian experiment. The amount of ruthless coercion that has gone into the making of the Russian industrial revolution is explained mainly by the rulers' determination to overcome at any cost the prodigious difficulties involved in the mobilization, training, and education of many millions of raw, undisciplined peasants. In a more highly developed economy with a disciplined and civilized industrial working class such methods would be not only superfluous—they would also be positively incompatible with an orderly planned economy. It is therefore reasonable to think that the planners would not feel themselves tempted to resort to them.

Such experience of planning as war-time Britain has had hardly supports the gloomy 'road-to-serfdom' prophecies. Surely, the amount of direction of labour introduced in war-time Britain did not seem to the working classes to be as oppressive as the uncertainty and misery of the booms and slumps of the preceding era. True enough, the worker was limited in his choice of a job or of the place of his work. This, however, was hardly more than an inconvenience greatly offset by the advantages of full and stable employment. It was, in part at least, as a result of this experience that, in the General Election of 1945, the British working classes opted for what they believed to be a policy shielding them from new slumps and unemployment. Yet in war-time Britain planning was also tried amid scarcity, although even that scarcity would still have looked like dazzling abundance to most Russians. Even in the Third Reich it was not planning that led to cruelty and atrocities but the Nazi ideology of the master race. Incidentally, we now know that, contrary to Nazi boasts, Germany in the Second World War was among those belligerent nations that were least advanced in planning.

Within a planned economy developing on a relatively high industrial and cultural basis considerable scope should be left for trade union activity. In Russia no bargaining was really possible between management and workers because of the extreme scarcity of all material resources. In a country producing, say, only one pair of shoes per year for every third citizen the worker could not effectively bargain over whether his wages should enable him to buy only one or two pairs of shoes per year. The trade unions could not adopt a 'consumptionist' attitude in any circumstances, although they need not perhaps have gone to extremes of anti-consumptionism. But in any economy possessing its safety margins in material wealth a degree of bargaining between management and workers would not only be compatible with planning but also essential to its effectiveness. Here the worker may try to improve his standard of living without necessarily thereby upsetting the balance of the plans or seriously hampering capital investment. Here the planners should be in a position to plan the distribution of the national income with a flexibility of which the Russians could not even dream. The freedom of bargaining may, of course, have to be restricted occasionally; but this need not be the rule. The question how often the need to restrict such freedom would arise depends on how wide or narrow are the safety margins of any national economy at any time. On the other hand, it must be expected that in the east, especially in a Communist China, which even to-day is more backward than was pre-revolutionary Russia, the main features of the Russian system will be reproduced, if rapid industrialization is attempted.

Nor is this merely a matter of the industrial resources with which a country embarks upon planned economy. Social custom and habit and the peculiarities of native civilizations play their part. The traditional outlook of any nation permeates the fabric of any new social organization that nation may adopt and lends to it its own colour. Soviet

Russia, with its public ownership and planned economy, has absorbed all the still fresh traditions of tsarist autocracy and serfdom. It was not planned economy that drove Russia on to the road of serfdom—the fact that Russia had hardly ever left that road for any length of time vitiated her planned economy. In countries with a deep-rooted tradition of liberty, their social and cultural climate should help them to evolve methods of planning so efficient and humane that by comparison the Russian experiment would appear what historically it is—the first barbarously clumsy and costly, and yet profoundly significant attempt of a nation to master the 'blind forces' of its economy.

STATUTE

of the Soviet Trade Unions adopted by the tenth Congress
of the Trade Unions of the U.S.S.R.

(27 April 1949)[1]

Under the leadership of the All-Union Communist Party (Bolsheviks)
the Soviet people has built the socialist society and is successfully fulfilling
the historic task of the gradual transition from socialism to communism.
In the Soviet Union the exploiting classes have been completely liquidated,
the exploitation of man by man has been abolished for ever, unemployment in town and poverty in the countryside have been eliminated, and
the material and cultural standard of life of the toilers has been considerably raised. From the heavy burden which it is under capitalism, labour
has in our country become a matter of honour, glory, valour, and heroism.
'With us people work not for the exploiters, not for the enrichment of
idlers, but for themselves, for their own class, for their own Soviet society,
where the best people of the working class wield power' (Stalin).

The world-historic achievements of the toilers of the Soviet Union are
made secure in the Constitution of the U.S.S.R.

The Constitution guarantees to all citizens of the Soviet Union the
right to work, the right to rest, the right to education, the right to material
security in old age, in case of illness and loss of capacity for work. The
woman in the U.S.S.R. enjoys equal rights with the man in all fields of
economic, governmental, cultural and social-political life.

Freedom of expression, freedom of the press, freedom of meetings, and
also the right to associate in social organizations are guaranteed by law to
the citizens of the U.S.S.R., in the interests of the toilers and for the
purpose of strengthening the socialist order.

The Soviet Trade Unions, being a social, non-party, mass organization,
unite on a voluntary basis the workers and employees of all occupations,
without difference of race, nationality, sex, or religious convictions.

The Soviet Trade Unions carry out their entire work under the leadership of the Communist Party—the organizing and directing force of
Soviet society. The Trade Unions of the U.S.S.R. rally the working masses
behind the party of Lenin-Stalin.

The Trade Unions strive to enhance in every way the socialist order in
society and State, the moral-political unity of the Soviet people, the
brotherly co-operation and friendship between the peoples of the Soviet

[1] *Trud*, 11 May 1949.

Union; they actively participate in the election of the organs of State power; they organize workers and employees for the struggle for the steady development of the national economy; they concern themselves with the further rise of the material well-being and with the full satisfaction of the cultural needs of the toilers.

The Trade Unions educate their members in the spirit of Soviet patriotism, of a Communist attitude towards labour and towards the community's socialist property; they work for the Communist education of the toilers and for the raising of their cultural and technical level to that of the highly skilled technical personnel; they cultivate in the members of the Trade Unions the sense of proletarian internationalism, fight for the unity of the international labour movement, for stable peace and democracy all over the world. The Trade Unions 'are an educational organization . . . a school of administration, a school of economic management, a school of communism' (Lenin).

In the conditions of the Soviet socialist order, the State defends the rights of the toilers, and its legislation expresses the interests of the people. The Trade Unions take an active part in preparing the laws concerning production, labour, the way of life and culture, and they fight for the steadfast realization of those laws.

The Trade Unions:

organize the socialist emulation of workers and employees for the fulfilment and overfulfilment of State plans, for the raising of labour productivity, improvement in the quality of production, and lowering of its cost;

participate in the planning and regulating of the wages of workers and employees, in working out various systems of wages, their socialist guiding principle being the payment of labour according to its quantity and quality; they strive to introduce new progressive norms of output and they see to it that labour should be correctly assessed and paid in piece-rates and progressing premiums;

help workers and employees to raise their productive and business qualifications; communicate to others the experience of advanced workers and employees, innovators of production and science, and assist in the diffusion of technical progress throughout industry;

conclude collective agreements with the administration of concerns;

exercise supervision over the state of labour protection and industrial security in enterprises and institutions; participate in the settlement of labour disputes; conclude agreements with the administration of concerns on the manner of utilization of funds allocated for measures of industrial safety and labour protection;

administer the business of State social insurance, fix the amount of allowances for temporary incapacity and pay them out to workers and employees, strive for a better organization of medical assistance to the toilers and of the protection of the health of women and children, set up sanatoria and rest homes, organize funds of mutual assistance, participate in the allocation of housing space in houses that belong to businesses and institutions, carry out mass control over the fulfilment of plans for the building of houses and cultural centres, over the work of communal dining rooms, magazines, communal cultural institutions, and urban transport;

assist members of the Trade Unions in raising their ideological-political and general educational level, spread political and scientific knowledge, and conduct broad propaganda on matters of productive technique; set up clubs, homes, and palaces of culture, Red corners, libraries, develop artistic mass activity, physical culture, sports, and tourism among the workers and employees;

help to attract women into public, productive, and social life and assist workers and employees in the Communist education of children;

act on behalf of the workers and employees *vis-à-vis* State and social bodies in matters concerning labour, culture, and the workers' way of life.

I. MEMBERS OF THE TRADE UNION, THEIR RIGHTS AND OBLIGATIONS

1. Every citizen of the U.S.S.R. working in an industrial business or in an office, or studying at a higher educational institution, technical and trade school can be a member of a Trade Union.

2. The member of a Trade Union *has the right*:

(a) to participate in the general meetings of members of the Trade Union;

(b) to elect and to be elected to all Trade Union bodies, to conferences and congresses of Trade Unions;

(c) to put before the Trade Union bodies questions and proposals concerning the improvement of Trade Union work;

(d) to criticize at Trade Union meetings, conferences, congresses, and in the press the activity of any local and higher Trade Union body and its workers, to address questions, statements, and complaints to any leading Trade Union body;

(e) to turn to the Trade Union for the defence and support of his or her rights in cases where the administration has offended against the collective agreement or the valid legislation on labour, social insurance, and welfare;

(f) to demand his or her personal participation in all cases in which a Trade Union body may take a decision affecting his or her activity or conduct.

3. A member of the Trade Union is *under the obligation:*

(a) to observe strictly State and labour discipline;

(b) to economize and enhance the community's socialist property as the sacred and inviolable basis of the Soviet order, as the source of the Fatherland's wealth and power, as the source of abundant and civilized life for all toilers;

(*c*) to improve his or her productive and business qualifications, to master the technique of his or her trade;

(*d*) to conform to the Statute of the Trade Union, to contribute regularly membership fees.

4. A member of the Trade Union enjoys the *following advantages*:

(*a*) receives from the funds of State social insurance higher allowances than those granted to non-members, in proportions fixed by legislation;

(*b*) obtains on a basis of priority travel facilities to rest homes, sanatoria, and resorts, and also travel facilities for children to kinder-gartens and Pioneers' camps; receives material assistance in case of need from Trade Union funds;

(*c*) is accorded by Trade Union bodies legal aid without payment;

(*d*) benefits personally from the cultural and sport institutions of the Trade Union on terms fixed by the Trade Union bodies; the member's family has the same right;

(*e*) has the right to become a member of the Trade Union's mutual assistance fund.

5. Admission to the Trade Union is granted after a personal application for membership. The decision as to admission is taken by the meeting of the Trade Union group and confirmed by the Trade Union shop-com-mittee, or—where a shop-committee is not in existence—by the factory or local committee. Where a Trade Union group does not exist admission to membership is decided by the general meeting of the members of the Trade Union.

6. The applicant becomes a member from the day on which the meeting of the Trade Union group or of the Trade Union organization of the shop, branch, business, or institution has decided to admit him or her. The factory or local committee of the Trade Union issues the membership card.

7. If the member of a Trade Union is transferred to a business or institution which comes under a different Trade Union, he or she becomes a member of that Trade Union without paying entrance fee and retains all acquired rights [which may depend on the duration of his membership].[1]

8. The time of members' service in the Armed Forces of the U.S.S.R. is included in their Trade Union *stage*.

9. Members who because of ill-health or old age have ceased to work and are paid pensions retain their right to remain in the ranks of the Trade Union.

10. Seasonal workers and employees retain their Trade Union *stage* if they resume work in the next season. Members of artels of industrial

[1] 'And retains, his or her *stage*' says the Russian original. The word *stage* is used to describe the duration of membership and the rights acquired according to that duration.

co-operation [that is of artisans' co-operatives] cannot at the same ɪme be members of Trade Unions. If they were members of a Trade Union before they joined an artel and if they then leave the artel to work in an industrial business or in an institution, their previous Trade Union *stage* is re-established.

11. For offences against the Statute of the Trade Union, failure to contribute member's fees in the course of more than three months, or undisciplined conduct, Trade Union bodies may impose upon a member of a Trade Union the following penalties: a warning, public censure, rebuke, and the extreme measure—expulsion from the Trade Union.

A decision of the shop-meeting or of the Trade Union group on expulsion from the Trade Union comes into effect after endorsement by the factory or local committee of the Trade Union. Any decision of a primary Trade Union organization on the imposition of a penalty on a member of a Trade Union is taken in his or her presence.

II. The Organizational Structure of Trade Unions

12. The Trade Unions are built on the foundations of democratic centralism as follows:

(*a*) all Trade Union bodies from bottom to top are elected by the members of the Trade Union and are accountable to them;

(*b*) Trade Union organizations decide on all matters concerning Trade Union work in accordance with the statute of the Trade Union and the decisions of higher Trade Union bodies;

(*c*) decisions of Trade Union organizations are adopted by a majority vote of the members of the Trade Union;

(*d*) lower Trade Union bodies are subordinate to the higher ones.

13. Trade Unions are organized on the production principle: all who work in one industrial concern or in one institution are united in one Trade Union; every Trade Union embraces workers and employees working in one branch of the national economy.

14. For the purpose of co-ordinating the activity of Trade Union organizations in regions, provinces, and republics, regional, provincial, and republican councils of Trade Unions are formed.

15. The highest leading body of any Trade Union organization is the general meeting (for primary organizations), the conference (for district, town, regional, provincial, and republican organizations), and the Congress (for the Trade Union as a whole).

The general meeting, the conference, or the Congress elect the appropriate committee, for the shop, factory, locality, district, town, region, province, republic, or the central committee, each committee being their executive organ and directing the entire current work of the organization.

16. All leading bodies of the Trade Unions, and also delegates to conferences and congresses, are elected by secret ballot.

At the election of Trade Union bodies, members of the Trade Union have the right to put forward candidates, to challenge and criticize any one of them.

The elected Trade Union bodies choose from among their own members the chairman, the secretary, and the members of the praesidium in an open ballot.

17. Elections to any Trade Union body may be carried out before the prescribed term on the demand of not less than one-third of the members of the Trade Union concerned and also on the decision of a higher Trade Union body.

18. General meetings of members, conferences, and congresses of Trade Unions, and also meetings of Trade Union committees and councils of Trade Unions are considered competent to take decisions if not less than two-thirds of the members of the Trade Union, delegates, or committee members participate.

19. Trade Union bodies are obliged to observe steadfastly Trade Union democracy: to call general meetings and conferences of members, to present reports and carry out elections, to create conditions favourable for the development of criticism and self-criticism in organizations, to attract members on a broad scale to participation in Trade Union activity, and to hold meetings of Trade Union *activists*.

20. Commissions for the various branches of Trade Union work are formed by the shop, factory, local, district, town, regional, and provincial committees, and by the councils of Trade Unions. Branches and sectors are formed by the All-Union Central Council of Trade Unions, central committees of Trade Unions, and also by republican, provincial, and regional councils and committees of Trade Unions.

III. Supreme Trade Union Authorities

21. The All-Union Congress of Trade Unions is the supreme authority of the Trade Unions of the U.S.S.R.

The All-Union Congress of Trade Unions:

(a) receives and endorses the reports of ACCTU (All-Union Central Council of Trade Unions) and of the Committee of Auditors;

(b) confirms the Statute of the Trade Unions of the U.S.S.R.;

(c) defines the tasks of the Trade Unions, receives the reports of the central economic organs, and suggests measures for the participation of Trade Unions in the struggle for the fulfilment and overfulfilment of national economic plans and for the raising of the material well-being and the cultural-political level of workers and employees;

(d) indicates the tasks of the Trade Unions of the U.S.S.R. in the international Trade Union movement;

(e) elects the All-Union Central Council of the Trade Unions and the Committee of Auditors.

146

22. The All-Union Congress of Trade Unions is convened at least once in four years. Notice of the Congress is given at least two months before the Congress.

23. The All-Union Central Council of Trade Unions directs the entire activity of the Trade Unions in the intervals between All-Union Congresses.

24. The All-Union Central Council of Trade Unions:

(*a*) defines the tasks of the Trade Union movement at large and also those concerning particular problems of Trade Union work;

(*b*) participates in the preparation of national economic plans;

(*c*) leads the socialist emulation;

(*d*) receives reports from the committees of the Trade Unions and also from ministries and departments on matters concerning production and the broad cultural work among workers and employees;

(*e*) prepares and submits to the consideration of the Government projects of laws concerning wages, protection of labour, social insurance, welfare, and cultural services; issues instructions, regulations, and rulings on the application of the existing labour legislation;

(*f*) manages the entire system of State social insurances;

(*g*) carries out All-Union cultural, sport, and other mass activities;

(*h*) creates Trade Union schools and training courses;

(*i*) confirms the budget of the Trade Unions;

(*j*) represents the Soviet Trade Unions in the international Trade Union movement and in international Trade Union associations;

(*k*) has it own press organ—the newspaper *Trud*—its own publishing concern (*Profizdat*), publishes Trade Union journals, bulletins, etc.

25. The All-Union Central Council of Trade Unions elects a praesidium and secretariat. Plenary sessions of ACCTU are convened regularly.

26. The supreme leading organ of any Trade Union is the Congress of that Trade Union. The Congress of a Trade Union is convened once in two years. Delegates to the Congress are elected by members of the Trade Union at meetings and conferences according to norms established by the central committee of the Trade Union. The central committee gives notice of the Congress at least one month before it is convened.

Members and alternate members of the central committee of the Trade Union and of the Commission of Auditors who have not been elected as delegates to the Congress participate in the Congress in an advisory capacity.

The Congress of the Trade Union receives reports on the activity of the central committee of the Trade Union and the Commission of Auditors, defines the successive tasks of the Trade Union, confirms the Statute of the Trade Union, receives reports of economic authorities on the course of the execution of the State plans, discusses matters concerning cultural and welfare services for the toilers, problems of the international Trade Union movement, elects the central committee of the Trade Union, the Commission of Auditors, and delegates to the All-Union Congress of Trade Unions.

An extraordinary Congress may be called by decision of the ACCTU or of the central committee of the Trade Union.

27. In the intervals between two Congresses the central committee directs the entire activity of the Trade Union.

The central committee of the Trade Union and the Commission of Auditors are elected for two years.

28. The central committee of the Trade Union:

organizes socialist emulation, draws up, together with the economic authorities, the balance sheet of the all-Union socialist emulation, receives their reports on the state of production, protection of labour, and industrial safety, organizes the campaigns for collective agreements and contracts on protection of labour, takes measures to improve the work of concerns, institutions, and Trade Union organizations as regards organization of labour, wages, socialist emulation, social insurance, welfare and cultural services for workers and employees;

confirms the Trade Union budget and the budget of the State social insurance and also reports on the execution of those budgets;

records collective agreements concluded by local Trade Union organizations with business managements;

fixes rules and norms concerning industrial safety, obligatory for the given branch of production;

organizes ideological-political education and training of Trade Union cadres;

conducts the Trade Union's publishing business (newspapers, journals, reports, etc.);

puts forward active members of the Trade Union for work in State, Soviet, economic, and social organizations;

determines the constitution of the central committee of the Trade Union and appoints the managers of the branches of the central committee of the Trade Union;

maintains and develops, through ACCTU, contact with the Trade Unions of foreign countries.

Plenary sessions of the central committee of the Trade Union are convened regularly.

The central committee elects its praesidium consisting of the chairman, secretary, and members of the praesidium to direct the daily work of the Trade Union.

The central committee of the Trade Union is responsible for its activity to the Congress of the Trade Union and to ACCTU.

IV. REPUBLICAN, PROVINCIAL, REGIONAL, TOWN, AND DISTRICT TRADE UNION BODIES

29. Regional, provincial, republican councils of Trade Unions and Commissions of Auditors are elected at the appropriate inter-Trade Union conferences for a term of two years.

Delegates to the inter-union conferences are elected at meetings of Trade Union members in industrial businesses, institutions, and educational establishments, the Trade Union organizations of which are directly subordinate to the central committees of the Trade Unions, and at town, district, regional, provincial, and republican conferences of branch Trade Unions.

30. Regional, provincial, and republican councils of Trade Unions
   are responsible for inter-union work;
   co-ordinate the joint activities of Trade Union organizations of the region, province, or republic, activities designed to develop socialist emulation for the fulfilment and overfulfilment of State plans by industrial concerns, to improve further the material well-being of workers and employees and the cultural services;
   study, generalize, and impart to others the advanced experience of Trade Union work;
   direct the work of the inter-union cultural and sports institutions.
   Plenary sessions of the council of the Trade Unions are convened regularly.

31. Republican, provincial, regional, main-railway, industrial basin, town, and district committees of Trade Unions and Commissions of Auditors are elected at conferences of the corresponding Trade Union convened once in two years.

The conference receives reports of the committee and the Commission of Auditors, discusses issues of Trade Union work, organization of labour and production, welfare and cultural services, elects leading Trade Union bodies, delegates to the Congress of the Trade Union and to the inter-union conference.

32. The committees guide the Trade Union organizations of the corresponding Trade Union on the scale of the republic, province, region, town, district, main-railway line, or industrial basin; they organize the execution by the Trade Union organizations of the decisions of ACCTU and of the central committee of the Trade Union, pass the budget estimates of primary Trade Union organizations, and conduct the meetings of the Trade Union *activists*. Plenary sessions of committees are convened regularly. In all their activity the committees are accountable to the corresponding republican, provincial, regional, town, district conference of members of the Trade Union and to the central committee of the Trade Union, and as regards inter-union activity in republics, provinces, and districts they are also accountable to the councils of Trade Unions.

33. The councils and committees of Trade Unions elect from their members chairmen, secretaries, and members of praesidiums.

V. PRIMARY TRADE UNION ORGANIZATIONS

34. Primary Trade Union organizations form the basis of the Trade Union. A primary organization consists of members of the Trade Unions

149

working in one industrial business or office. The general meeting of Trade Union members is the highest organ of the primary Trade Union organization.

In industrial businesses and in institutions where it is impossible to convene general meetings, either because the work is done in many shifts or because of the territorial dispersal of shops and sectors, shift meetings or shift conferences of members are convened.

35. The tasks of the primary Trade Union organization consist in:

(a) mobilizing all workers and employees of the business or institution for the fulfilment and overfulfilment of the production plan, for the strengthening of labour discipline, and development of socialist emulation;

(b) attracting all workers and employees to the Trade Union and carrying out political-educational work among them;

(c) fulfilling obligations arising out of the collective agreement;

(d) preparing practical measures designed to raise productivity of labour, to improve quality of output, to enforce strict financial accountancy within every shop and working brigade, to lower the cost of production, and to raise the profitability of the enterprise; conducting production meetings and supervising the execution of their decisions; co-operating in the utilization of suggestions for the rationalization of labour;

(e) organizing Stakhanovite schools and the guardianship of old and regular workers and the technical personnel over new workers, organizing lessons and lectures on advanced methods of work and in other ways assisting workers and employees in fulfilling and overfulfilling norms of output and in raising their productive skill;

(f) day-to-day care for the improvement of labour conditions and for workers' and employees' welfare;

(g) satisfying the cultural needs of workers and employees and promoting mass cultural and sport activity;

(h) giving effect to decisions adopted by higher Trade Union bodies and general meetings.

36. For the purpose of conducting current work the primary Trade Union organization, consisting of no fewer than twenty-five members, elects the factory or local committee and a Commission of Auditors, and a Trade Union organization consisting of fewer than twenty-five members elects a trade organizer for a term of one year.

The numerical strength of a factory and local committee and of the Commission of Auditors is determined by the general meeting or the conference of Trade Union members.

The factory and local committee concludes the collective agreement with the management of the establishment and organizes mass check-ups on its fulfilment; it conducts the work of production meetings; it encourages inventions and projects for rationalization of labour coming from the mass of workers; confirms the composition of the commissions and council of social insurance; convenes general meetings and conferences; organizes the execution of decisions of higher Trade Union bodies; induces members of the Trade Union to take an active part in social work.

37. In the shops of any establishment shop-committees are formed by decision of the factory committee, and in the branches and offices of institutions Trade Union bureaux are formed by decision of the local committee; and these are elected for one year.

The shop-committees and the Trade Union bureaux organize the entire Trade Union work within the shops and branches, secure the execution of the decisions of the factory and local committee and of higher Trade Union bodies, conduct meetings of workers and employees, form trade groups, and direct the work of the trade group organizers.

38. Trade Union groups are formed in order to take better care of Trade Union members working in the same brigade, at the same bench, aggregate, sector, etc.

At the general meeting of the Trade Union group the organizer of the group (*Profgruporg*) is elected for one year in open ballot. The trade group elects, from its members, an insurance delegate and a social inspector for protection of labour to assist the group organizer.

The group organizer induces all workers to join the Trade Union, collects membership fees, organizes socialist emulation and assists the factory, local, and shop committees in taking measures concerning the welfare and the cultural needs of workers and employees.

VI. TRADE UNION FUNDS

39. The funds of the Trade Unions consist of entrance and monthly membership fees, income from cultural-educational and sports institutions, auxiliary enterprises, houses, and premises, and other sources.

40. Monthly membership fees amount to 1 per cent of actual monthly earnings, and for students, of their monthly stipends. Such members of the Trade Union as non-working pensioners and students who do not receive any stipend pay a membership fee of 1 rouble a month.

41. Entrance fees, paid on admission, amount to 1 per cent of the wage or stipend received, and for students not receiving stipends, 1 rouble.

42. The funds of ACCTU consist of sums deducted by the central committee of the Trade Union from the membership fees they receive, in proportions fixed by ACCTU, and of other returns.

43. Republican, provincial, and regional councils of Trade Unions are financed by ACCTU, according to approved estimates.

44. The financial means of Trade Unions are used to provide cultural services and material assistance to members and to finance organizational and economic activities of Trade Union bodies. The allocation of funds is decided upon by the central committees at their annual budgetary sessions

and by ACCTU when it passes the compound budget of the Trade Unions.

Trade Union bodies spend their funds in accordance with estimates approved by higher Trade Union bodies.

ACCTU, central, republican, provincial, regional, and also factory and local committees of the Trade Unions publish their financial accounts for the information of Trade Union members.

45. The right to dispose of the financial means and property of the Trade Unions belongs to elected Trade Union bodies, which are responsible for the timely levying of funds, preservation of property, and correct utilization of funds.

Redistribution of property within one Trade Union may be carried out by decision of the central committee of that Trade Union, and between various Trade Unions—by decision of ACCTU.

46. Commissions of Auditors of Trade Unions elect chairmen and secretaries from their members. The Commissions audit the accounts and the execution of the Trade Union budget, the budget of State social insurance, the correctness and expediency of expenditure, and the use made of Trade Union property.

Commissions of Auditors report on their activity to congresses, conferences, and general meetings simultaneously with other Trade Union bodies.

VII. The Rights of Trade Union Bodies as Legal Persons

47. Factory, local, town, district, trunk-line, basin, regional, provincial, republican, and central committees of the Trade Unions, and also ACCTU and republican, provincial, regional councils of Trade Unions are legal persons. They have their stamp and seal in a form fixed by the corresponding central committee of the Trade Union and ACCTU.

48. Every branch Trade Union has its statute, reflecting the peculiarities of that Trade Union and conforming to the Statute of the Trade Unions of the U.S.S.R.

The statute of every Trade Union must be registered with ACCTU.

INDEX

All-Union (All-Russian) Central Council of Trade Unions (ACCTU) *see* Trade Unions

All-Russian Congress of Producers, 54, 55

Anarchists, 18

Andreev, 63, 122 *n*

Arbitration, 72, 73

Auditors, Commission of, 146, 147 *et seq.*

Blanqui, 5

Bukharin, 43, 44, 52, 76, 80

Central Committee of Communist Party, 57, 111

Central Council of Trade Unions *see* Trade Unions

Central Executive Committee of Soviets, 22

Coal industry, 113

Collective agreements, 125, 129-30, 132, 142

Collective farms, 85, 86

Collectivization, 75

Comintern, 64

Communist Party, vii, 2, 5, 9, 10, 11, 13, 14, 21, 24, 29, 53, 54, 75

Programme, 28-33, 46

relations with Trade Unions, vii, 4, 6, 10, 28-9, 31-3, 64, 65

Communist Party Congresses, 33, 42-52, 59, 60, 62, 64, 65, 71, 73, 80, 96, 98, 105, 116

Constitution of U.S.S.R., 141

Cultural and Educational Activities, Commission for, 124

Democracy, proletarian, 52-8, 75

Dictatorship, proletarian, 52-8

Dogadov, 69, 71

Donetz Basin, 90, 107, 108

'Economists', 2, 3, 7, 8

Education, Commissariat of, 94

Factory Committees, 15, 16, 17-18, 54, 86, 123-7

Factory schools, 94, 95

First International, 2

Five-Year Plans, 66, 79, 81-2, 101, 103, 117, 134

Glavki, 28

Gorbunov, S., 133

Health, 118

Housing Commission, 124

Industrial management, 33-42, 45, 62

Industrialization, 75, 76, 77, 79, 84

Industrial recruitment, 84

Iskra, 6

Kaganovich, 80

Kamenev, 70, 75, 76

Kerensky Government, 13, 14

Kronstadt rising, 53

Kuibyshev, 79

Kuznetsov, V. V., 128, 130, 131, 134

Labour armies, 33–42
  Commissariat of, 24, 26, 27, 31, 45, 50, 73, 107, 116
  fluidity of, 87–93
  Laws, Code of, 30
  protection, 119, 125, 142
  protection commission, 124
  training of, 93–6
Lassalle, 3
Left Social Revolutionaries, 59
Lenin, differences with Trotsky, 56
  on individual management in industry, 34
  on social democracy, 6–7
  on trade unions, 2–8, 11, 14, 20, 26–7, 43, 48, 49–51, 56, 57, 58, 142
  on wages policy, 51
'Liquidators', 10
Lozovsky, 20, 21, 22, 60

Maisky, 14, 19
Martov, 19, 20, 56
Marx, Marxism, 4, 39, 40, 97, 110
Mensheviks, 2, 5, 9, 10, 11, 13, 14, 15, 18, 19, 36, 60
Miliutin, 52, 60
Miners Trade Union, 107, 132
Molotov, 90, 108, 116

NEP (New Economic Policy), 59–74, 75, 121, 122
Norms and Conflicts Commission, 107, 125

Orjonikidze, 79
Osoaviakhim, 120

Piece-work, 107–9
Planned economy, 75–120, 135–40
'Platform of Ten', 43, 48

Popova, N. V., 128
Pravda, 113
Private enterprise, 67, 68, 69, 75
Producers, All-Russian Congress of, 54, 55
Production meetings, 126, 133
Productivity, 79, 100, 101, 111, 112, 142
Profgrup, 125–6, 133
Profintern, 20
Profizdat, 147
Proletarian democracy, 52–8, 75
  dictatorship, 52–8

RKK *see* Norms and Conflicts Commission
Red Army, 25, 36, 50
Red Trade Union International *see* Profintern
Revolutions, 1905, 8–12, 13
  1917, 13
Rudzutak, 72
Ryazanov, 20
Rykov, 76, 80

Sanatoria, 113, 117, 143
Schmidt, 24, 27–8, 68, 72, 73, 80
Servicemen's Families, Commission for Assistance to, 124
Shlyapnikov, A., 43, 54, 55, 57
Shock-work, 99, 109
Shop committees, 125, 134
Shvernik, 80, 90, 116
Social Democracy, Lenin's views on, 6–7
Social Democratic Workers' Party, 2, 3, 5, 8
  Congresses, 2, 9, 10
  relations with Trade Unions, 10–11
Social Insurance, 116–20, 133, 134, 142
  Council of, 124

'Socialist emulation', 96–9, 109, 142

Social Revolutionaries, 13, 18

Soviets, 8, 9, 13, 15, 21
    Central Executive Committee of, 22

Stakhanovism 109–16, 118

Stalin, 1, 36, 39, 77, 90, 98, 105, 108, 116, 141

State Labour Reserves, 85, 95

Statute of Soviet Trade Unions, 141–52

Strikes, 61, 68, 72, 73, 77, 88

Supreme Council of National Economy, 28, 31, 35, 44, 45, 52, 71, 76, 94

Tambov rising, 53

Tomsky, Mikhail, 18, 26, 41, 57, 63, 71, 72, 74, 75, 76, 77–8, 80, 104

Trade Union Congresses, vii
    First, 18–25
    Second, 26, 27, 121
    Third, 33, 36, 43
    Fourth, 52, 59–60, 103
    Fifth, 61, 71, 72
    Seventh, 69, 104, 121
    Eighth, 68, 77, 80, 104
    Ninth, 127
    Tenth, 127, 128–34

Trade Unions
    All-Union (All-Russian) Central Council of, 21, 22, 28, 32, 33, 41, 44, 45, 50, 57, 60, 63, 72, 94, 117, 118, 127, 128, 132, 146–7
    in the Civil War, 25–8
    relations with Communist Party, vii, 4, 6, 10, 28–9, 31–3, 64, 65
    Councils, 131–2
    funds, 151–2
    and industrialization, 76, 77, 79
    leadership, 128–9, 146–8
    legal status, 152

Lenin's views on, 2–8, 11, 14, 20, 26–7, 43, 48, 49–51, 56, 57, 58, 142
    machinery and organization of, 121–7, 145–6
    membership, 13, 25, 121, 122
    and NEP, 66–74
    in the 1905 Revolution and after, 8–12
    in the 1917 Revolution and after, 13–58
    number of, 51, 121
    and Planned Economy, 81–120
    press, 147
    primary organizations, 149–51
    republican, provincial, regional, town, and district bodies, 148–9
    rights and obligations of members, 143–5
    and social insurance, 116–20
    statification of, 45, 48, 60
    Statute, 141–52
    and workers' control, 14–15, 16

Transport, Central Committee of, 41–2

Trotsky, 34, 35, 36–8, 39, 40, 41, 42, 43–4, 45, 48, 49, 55, 56, 58, 70, 73, 75, 76, 96

Trud, 147

Tsektran, 41, 42

Tsyperovich, 24

Udarnichestvo, see shock-work

Unemployment, 67, 68, 83

Voprosy Truda, 107

VSNKh see Supreme Council o National Economy

Wages, commissions, 124, 133
    policy, 45, 47, 51, 68, 71, 96, 98, 99, 100–9, 131
    scales, 104–7, 109, 110, 112–13, 142

Welfare *see* Social Insurance
Workers' control of industry, 14, 15, 25
Workers' Delegates, Council of, 8, 9
Workers' Inventions and Rationalization, Commission of, 124
Workers' Opposition, 46–8, 53, 54, 55, 58, 60

Workers' Supply Department, 120, 124

Zhdanov, 79, 115, 116
Zinoviev, 21, 22, 54, 70, 73, 75, 76
Zubatov, Colonel, 1